PRAISE FOR
GOTTLAND

"An intelligent, captivating, and much-needed book."
—ADAM MICHNIK

"A great book. Mariusz Szczygieł is well versed in the Polish
school of reportage writing and he applies his method to this
specific Czech ambiguity. Original and surprising."
—AGNIESZKA HOLLAND

"Extraordinary, hypnotizing, and disturbing tales."
—LIBÉRATION

"If you want to understand the Czech Republic in
the twentieth century, read Gottland."
—FRANKFURTER ALLEGEMEINE ZEITUNG

"Masterful prose ... Impressive."
—NEUE ZÜRCHER ZEITUNG

"One of the most valuable and eloquent
testimonies about the Czech people."
—PRÁVO (CZECH REPUBLIC)

GOTTLAND

GOTTLAND

MOSTLY TRUE STORIES FROM HALF OF CZECHOSLOVAKIA

MARIUSZ SZCZYGIEŁ

Translated by Antonia Lloyd-Jones

MELVILLE HOUSE

BROOKLYN • LONDON

GOTTLAND: MOSTLY TRUE STORIES FROM HALF OF CZECHOSLOVAKIA

First published in Poland as *Gottland*
Copyright © 2006, 2014 by Mariusz Szczygieł
Translation copyright © 2014 by Antonia Lloyd-Jones

First Melville House printing: May 2014

Melville House Publishing   8 Blackstock Mews
  145 Plymouth Street   and   Islington
  Brooklyn, NY 11201   London N4 2BT

mhpbooks.com   facebook.com/mhpbooks   @melvillehouse

Library of Congress Cataloging-in-Publication Data

Szczygiel, Mariusz, 1966–
  [Gottland. English]
  Gottland : mostly true stories from half of Czechoslovakia /
Mariusz Szczygiel ; translated by Antonia Lloyd-Jones.
    pages   cm
  Originally published in Polish in 2006.
  Includes bibliographical references.
  ISBN 978-1-61219-313-7 (hardcover)
  ISBN 978-1-61219-314-4 (ebook)
  1. Czech Republic—Anecdotes. 2. Czech Republic—Social
conditions—Anecdotes. I. Lloyd-Jones, Antonia, translator. II.
Title.
DB2011.S9313 2014
943.71—dc23
                                                    2014012465

Design by Christopher King

Printed in the United States of America
          1 3 5 7 9 10 8 6 4 2

PUBLICATION SUBSIDIZED BY
THE POLISH BOOK INSTITUTE

BOOK INSTITUTE

THE ©POLAND
TRANSLATION
PROGRAM

©POLAND

CONTENTS

TIME LINE

Before the First World War, the Czech state
is known as Bohemia, and is part of the
Austro-Hungarian Empire.

1918 After the First World War, Czechoslovakia is
formed as an independent country.
The first president is Tomáš Garrigue
Masaryk.

1938 Nazi Germany annexes Sudetenland, an area
with a mainly German-speaking population.

1939 World War II—the Czech state is occupied
by Germany. It is called the Protectorate
of Bohemia and Moravia, and administered
by Reichsprotektor Reinhard Heydrich.

1942 Heydrich is assassinated by the Czech
resistance.

1945 Soviet and US armies liberate Czechoslovakia.

1945–46 The minority German population—three
million people—is expelled from the
country.

1948 The "Victorious February" takeover by
the communists. Klement Gottwald is the
country's president.

Early 1950s	A period of Stalinist repression.
1968	As leader of the Prague Spring, Alexander Dubček tries to introduce "socialism with a human face."
1968, December	Soviet and other Warsaw Pact troops invade to crush the Prague Spring. Dubček is replaced by hard-line communist Gustáv Husák.
1969	The introduction of repressive "normalization." Jan Palach and other human "torches" self-immolate in central Prague in protest.
1977	The dissident movement publishes Charter 77.
1989, November	The peaceful Velvet Revolution, led by the Civic Forum political movement, restores democracy. Former dissident playwright Václav Havel is the first president of the newly independent country.
1993	The country splits into the Czech Republic and Slovakia.
2004	The Czech Republic joins the European Union.

GOTTLAND

NOT A STEP WITHOUT BATA

For Egon Erwin Kisch

1882: A STINK

"Why does it smell so bad in here?" six-year-old Tomáš Bata*
asks his father, Antonín. This is the first manifestation of his
desire to set reality straight.

We do not know what his father says in reply. He is probably quite reticent on the whole.

Cobbler Antonín Bata is married for the second time.
Twice he has taken a widow with children as his wife. With
each wife he has also had his own children. Altogether, at his
small cobbler's workshop in Zlín he is raising twelve children
from four marriages. Apart from that, he works with seven
other people. His second wife does not like drafts.

TWELVE YEARS LATER: DEMANDS

The three children from his first marriage, Anna, Antonín
and eighteen-year-old Tomáš, are standing in front of their
fifty-year-old father. They are demanding their mother's in-
heritance. They're also suggesting that he should immediately

---

* In fact, the family name is spelled "Baťa," but as its customers became used
to "Bata," I decided to leave it in this, its globally familiar form.

give them whatever they are going to inherit after his death. They don't have the time to wait all those years, and anyway it is crowded at home.

They get eight hundred gulden in silver coins, and they hire four workers.

ONE YEAR LATER, 1895: THE PRINCIPLE

They have debts of eight thousand zlotys. They can't afford new leather hides and they have no money to pay for the old ones. Antonín is called up for the army, and Anna goes to work in Vienna as a domestic servant.

Tomáš stares at the remaining leather, and in his despair he hits upon the most important principle of his life: always turn failure into advantage.

As they cannot afford leather, they will have to make shoes out of what is available: canvas. Canvas doesn't cost much, and the rest of the leather can be used to make soles. This is how Bata devises one of the great successes of the new century: canvas shoes with leather soles. He brings in several thousand orders from Vienna, all gathered in a single day. People start to call the shoes *batovky*.

This allows him to build his first small factory, where fifty men work in a space of two thousand square feet.

1904: QUESTIONS

The workers notice that he can never be calm. He is always so stimulated that other people feel exhausted in his company.

He reads a newspaper article about some machines being

made in America. He sets off for the States, and in Lynn, Massachusetts, a shoe-making city, he hires himself out as a worker at a large factory. He takes three of his employees with him, and each one finds employment at a different place. He gives them orders to monitor each stage of production closely. Every Saturday the four shoemakers from Zlín meet up at a saloon, where they exchange observations.

They are amazed that, in America, even small children do their best to earn their own keep. What makes the biggest impression on Bata is a six-year-old boy who goes from house to house, catching flies in exchange for payment.

Some people are dying of poverty, but others bake fritters in the street and sell them for one cent. Tomáš notices a curious feature of the Americans: they can adapt en masse to any kind of novelty humanity has managed to invent.

He has brought 688 questions with him to the States, to which he seeks the answers. During his stay he adds seventy more questions. He reaches the conclusion that the standard of living of the average American, which is higher than in Europe, is due to being free of any kind of routine.

("It's clear that Tomáš Bata was an industrial spy in the USA," Czechoslovak historians will write sixty years later.)

1905: TEMPO

Tomáš learns more and more English, and hears something about Henry Ford. This employer, as E. L. Doctorow wrote of him, has long been convinced that most people are too stupid to be able to earn enough for a decent life. So he hit upon an idea. He divided the assembly of a car into separate, simple operations, which even an idiot would be capable of performing. Instead of teaching one worker hundreds of tasks, he decided to stand him in one spot and give him one and the same task to perform, all day long, and send the parts along a conveyor belt. This way the worker's mind would be unburdened. (It would take Ford several more years to put this idea into action.)

In the United States, Tomáš Bata comes across the term "wristwatch" for the first time. It has been in use for four years. With the beginning of the twentieth century the Americans have started to count time in minutes, and time has become the basic measure of production. "Productivity" and "American tempo"—the new fetishes—have demarcated the day into equal units of time. The working day has ceased to depend on the rising and setting of the sun.

SEPTEMBER 5, 1905: SECONDS

That night his father dies.

Tomáš returns to Zlín—still a squalid little town of the kind the Czechs describe as "where the bread ends and the stone begins"—and paints a large sign on the wall of his factory: THERE ARE 86,400 SECONDS IN A DAY. People read the sign and start to say that old Bata's son has lost his wits.

1905–1911: TOIL

He buys German and American machinery. The factory has six hundred workers by now. He builds the first residential housing for them.

When, in 1908, Ford issues his "car for Everyman" series, Tomáš is filled with excitement: "Ford is already making use of his production line!"

In America it takes seven hours to produce a single pair of shoes, and in France it takes almost six. On the wall of the rubber unit, Tomáš writes in letters six feet high: PEOPLE THINK, MACHINES TOIL!

At Bata, it only takes four hours to make a single pair of shoes now. Cobblers all over Moravia are devastated. Tomáš builds a brick wall around his factory, and has the following message inscribed on it: IT'S NOT PEOPLE WE FEAR, IT'S OURSELVES. (For over twenty years he will ignore this principle. It will never cross his mind that he will end his life a victim of his own self.)

1911: LOVE
He falls in love and proposes. He breaks off the engagement when his fiancée reveals to him that she can't have children.

JANUARY 1912: MAŇA
He goes to the famous Czech ball in Vienna; by now he is a well-known shoemaker who exports his shoes to the Balkans and Asia Minor. He is hoping to meet his future wife at the ball. He is attracted to Maňa Menčíková, daughter of the curator of the Imperial Library. The girl plays the piano and speaks three languages. Tomáš knows there has to be a written contract for everything. He sends a friend to ask the young lady whether she would sign a memorandum to

this effect: if she were not able to have children, they would divorce.

"So what benefit may I demand of him if I fail to satisfy his hopes?" replies the future Marie Batová. (After two years of trying for a child without success, Marie secretly buys a bottle of poison.)

DECEMBER 1913: THE LITTLE BOTTLE
For several months they have been living in a new villa, which Tomáš built before the wedding, so that his wife wouldn't feel any difference between life in Vienna and life in Zlín. When orders increase and the factory has to operate at night, Marie pours lemonade for the workers and hands out sandwiches. On returning home, she sometimes wonders whether a tree that doesn't produce fruit should be cut down, and glances at the little bottle.

JUNE 28, 1914: WAR
In Sarajevo, the life of Archduke Franz Ferdinand comes to an end. Austria announces mobilization.

The most eminent Czech of the twentieth century, professor of philosophy Tomáš Garrigue Masaryk, deputy to the Viennese parliament, comes back from vacation. "As I was on my way to Prague, I saw our people answering the call-up—in horror, as if going to the slaughter," he will say later. He has pangs of conscience. "Our people are off to the army and to prison, while we deputies sit at home."

Tomáš Bata is horrified: all his factory workers must

report for the war being fought by the Austro-Hungarian monarchy. Next morning, over his coffee, bacon and eggs, he has an idea: he will go to Vienna and extract an order for boots for the army. He leaves his eggs, gets in a horse-drawn cab, and races to the railway station at Otrokovice near Zlín. But the train has already left. So he buys the horses from the coachman and tells him to chase after the train. The animals rush as fast as the express through three villages, but in the fourth they collapse. In only six minutes Tomáš buys another cab and horses. He catches up with the train, and in a few hours he reaches Vienna.

In his opinion, one should never give in to reality, but always make skillful use of it for one's own purposes. In the course of two days, he secures an order for half a million pairs of boots and a guarantee that his workers won't go to the war.

His deal struck, he has seven minutes left to catch the train home; meanwhile a police unit is already rounding up his workers as deserters. On the way to the station, the cab in which Tomáš is riding gets into an accident, so the passenger jumps out and runs the rest of the way. He boards an express train to Brno.

He also gives work to laborers and cobblers who aren't employed at his factory. Even to those who used to be his sworn enemies. He saves the entire district from going to the front.

Towards the end of the war, in spite of the crisis, he will have almost five thousand workers, who will produce ten thousand pairs of army boots each day.

Marie Batová has long since forgotten the little bottle of poison which she bought before Christmas, and her decision that, if the eleventh course of treatment by the eighth doctor failed, she would commit suicide.

The last doctor had advised that impregnation could not happen in Zlín, and that Tomáš Bata would have to be away from his own terrain. So they went to the Krkonoše Mountains for ten days. (Nobody believed that Bata could endure so many days without inspecting the production line.)

As the shoemaker leaves his eggs and bacon and runs for the train, his wife is already in the seventh month of her pregnancy.

JANUARY 17, 1914: TOMÍK

Bata's son Tomáš is born, known as Tomík to differentiate him from his father.*

1918: BATA-IZATION

The war ends and the Czechoslovak state is founded. A large part of it has been "Bata-ized" for some time now.

"Tomáš established branches of Bata in almost every Moravian village, and as a result soon there was hardly anyone working privately as a cobbler in Bohemia, Moravia, Silesia, or Slovakia. Made-to-measure shoes became a thing of the past. Later on, Bata founded his own chain of workshops for shoe repair, and the profession of cobbler disappeared entirely," writes the communist reporter Egon Erwin Kisch.

Bata defends himself: "The Earth has two billion inhabit-

---

* Tomík Bata died on September 1, 2008.

ants," he keeps saying. "Each year, only nine hundred million pairs of shoes are produced in the entire world. Each person needs two pairs a year at the very least. An ambitious shoemaker is presented with the opportunity to sell a billion pairs of shoes. It's all just a question of price and the degree of civilization."

1919: RUMOR

They say (here I quote Kisch) there was a cobbler from Ostrava who, when he realized he had been completely ruined by Bata, packed his old workshop, dating back to the seventeenth century, into two cases and sent them to Bata's factory, straight to the boss. Then he, his wife and their two children jumped into the river.

Tomáš Bata, who received the news of this desperate step and the legacy at one and the same time, declared: "Put a sign above it to say that this is a cobbler's workshop from when I started working."

1920: A HUMAN BEING

Six-year-old Tomík goes to school barefoot. His father wants him to be no different from his schoolmates from Zlín.

The father sets up new production lines so that "each human unit is automatically driven to the greatest productivity." If any single worker cannot keep pace in the production line, the conveyor belt stops and a red bulb lights up on the wall. Thanks to this signaling system, the entire unit can see not only that they must stop work, but also who is to blame.

"In my work I do not only think about building factories, but people. What I do involves building the human being," notes Tomáš.

1921: LEAFLET

Rumors go round that Bata is in a mental hospital. One of the newspapers even publishes its address. Then, suddenly, leaflets appear all over Czechoslovakia, with the words:

> I AM NOT RICH
> I AM NOT POOR
> I AM NOT BANKRUPT
> I PAY GOOD WAGES
> I PAY ALL MY TAXES HONESTLY
> I MAKE GOOD SHOES
> PLEASE BELIEVE ME
> TOMÁŠ BATA.

EARLY 1922: CRISIS

In Europe, the post-war economic crisis continues for a third year, and there is galloping inflation, but Czechoslovakia manages to raise the value of the crown from six to eighteen U.S. cents. The country's position vis-à-vis its creditors is growing stronger, yet its companies now have debts abroad. Bata has warehouses packed with goods, and his customers need shoes, but they have no money.

Each month the company sells as much as it has produced in four days. For the other twenty-six days it might as well not be working.

Tomáš refuses to fight for tax relief. He also thinks it would be wrong to lay off any of his workers, because they will immediately demand unemployment benefits from the young state.

Other factories have already thrown out thousands of workers. It bothers him that the unemployed will now definitely not be able to afford his shoes. The value of the German mark falls, and the country is flooded by German shoes, growing cheaper from one day to the next.

AUGUST 29, 1922: CHEAPER

One morning, there's a shock: posters appear on the walls showing a fist thumping the words "High Prices" and announcing that from today onwards, the price of Bata's shoes has been almost halved. The shoes that used to cost 220 Czechoslovak crowns can now be bought for 119.

He tells the workers that you cannot overcome a major crisis by taking tiny steps.

He reduces their pay by 40 percent, but he doesn't lay anybody off. He pledges that the food in the factory stores will only be sold at token prices. As the value of the crown isn't rising, on their reduced pay they will live almost as well as before.

Customers rush to buy his shoes. He sells all the reserve stock in three months.

Of course he knows that the price reduction means immense losses for the factory, but it is the only way he can acquire hard cash. Moreover, this cash already has three times greater purchasing power, so he uses it to buy three times more materials.

Other firms lower their prices too, but by now it's too late. Bata was the first to do it. The newspapers write about Bata's seemingly illogical, but brilliant reaction to the strengthening of the crown.

Success. A year later Tomáš Bata will take on 1,800 new workers at the factory and will be elected *starosta* (mayor) of the city of Zlín.

MAY 1924: THE HAT

Ten-year-old Tomík travels to Brno with his parents in an open car. His hat is blown off by the wind. The car stops, and the boy runs to fetch it. He comes back and hears his father say: "I told you you've got to be careful. If that happens again we'll drive off without you."

Ten minutes later, the hat is blown off again. Tomáš Bata tells the driver to stop the car, gives his son ten crowns, and says: "Go to the railroad station and take the train to Brno. You can ride in the car with us on the way home."

However, the father must resign himself to going home without his son. The boy reaches Brno on time, goes into a Bata shoe store, borrows money from the cashier, and takes the train back to Zlín on his own.

1925: CHECKS

When Tomík graduates from elementary school at the age of eleven, his parents send him to high school in London. He goes there with his own checkbook, and his father opens an account for him at the Guaranty Trust Company of New

York. To pay his tuition fees, the boy presents checks to the proprietor of the school. At this elite school, the teenager from Czechoslovakia causes a sensation.

At the age of fourteen, he goes back to Zlín and—in keeping with his father's wishes—becomes a worker on the lowest wage. By now he can wear shoes.

When he is eighty-eight, I will ask his American secretary whether I may ask him some questions. "Yes," she replies. "Best to ask just one question, and to make it an important one."

I send it by e-mail: "Dear Mr. Bata, what's the best way to live?"

"You must study hard," replies Mr. Bata. "Look around you with your eyes open. Never repeat your mistakes, and draw conclusions from them. Work honestly and not just for your own profit. I don't think that's so difficult, is it?"

1925: BATAMAN

Tomáš Bata founds his first school. He does it out of compulsion, "because," he explains, "there are no known cases of the best educators in the country becoming millionaires. Usually they are paupers."

He advertises that he will accept six hundred boys aged fourteen for the next school year, and so his School for Young Men comes into being. A student at the school must finance himself. For eight hours a day, he earns enough in the factory for his food, board and clothing, and for four hours, he studies. Any sort of financial help from parents is forbidden. Each week, the student receives 120 crowns, spends seventy, and saves the rest in his own account. It is all worked out so that when, at the age of twenty-four, the young man returns to Bata from military service, he will have 100,000 crowns in his account. Tutors at the boarding houses keep track of booklets recording the students' expenditures. They also watch over the boys to make sure they keep their hands above their quilts. They are all given talks about hygiene and masturbation.

Emil Zátopek, the world's top athlete of 1952, keeps his hands above the quilt. Others who will do so too include: the famous (forty years on) writer Ludvík Vaculík, and the leading representative of the new wave in Czechoslovak cinema (also, forty years on) director Karel Kachyňa. Kachyňa starts work at Bata as a cleaner, and finishes as a trained draughtsman. "I was a Bataman," he'll say, in the early twenty-first century. "At Zlín I learned to fight against fear."

Each of Bata's students is a Bataman.

You can become a Bataman through obedience and hard work.

SEPTEMBER 1926: MILK

Tomáš is feeling pleased: he never went beyond elementary school, and has no title apart from "Chief" on his office door, but he's the author of a handbook entitled *Affluence for All*.

Tomáš Bata's Academy of Commerce is established.

Tomáš Bata slams his shoe against the desk when one of the students uses the money he has earned to drive all the way to Prague for a performance by the American dancer Josephine Baker—pioneer of the striptease.

From then on, neither students nor workers are allowed

to sit around in bars; drinking any sort of alcohol within the boundaries of Zlín is forbidden. Milk is recommended.

1926–1929: CHESS
Eight years after the Great October Revolution, Tomáš Bata initiates his experiments with capitalist society. He builds the citizens of Zlín an eight-story Community Center with a hotel (after the war, it will become the Hotel Moskva). He gives orders for there to be no café or wine bar on the ground floor next to the restaurant, just a big hall with table tennis, a bowling alley and a chess room ("because one should never stop thinking").

His people will no longer work eight hours, from 7 a.m. to 3 p.m.

Now they will work until 5 p.m., but at noon they will have a two-hour break. At that point the women can go home and make dinner, though Bata can't see why they would, when he has built large canteens and a department store that sells everything. "Women," he says in a speech, "you won't even have to make preserves—Bata will make them for you."

During the break the men and women can do what they like, but the following are recommended:

1. lying on the lawns in *Práce* [Labor] Square (in good weather);
2. not succumbing to idleness (so it is best to read, but with one reservation: DO NOT READ RUSSIAN NOVELS, says a slogan thought up by Bata and posted on the wall of the felting unit. Why not? Bata's reply is on

the wall of the rubber unit: RUSSIAN NOVELS KILL
YOUR JOIE DE VIVRE);

3. making use of the movie theater when the weather is
   bad (because Bata has already set up the biggest movie
   theater in Central Europe downtown, seating three
   thousand, with tickets costing one token crown);

4. compensating for falling behind at work—during the
   break, the incompetent are to make up for their ar-
   rears at the machines.

The trade unions and the Czechoslovak Communist Party
claim that this is the real reason Bata thought up the break—
to gain extra unpaid labor. Strikes are suppressed, and people
are thrown out of the factory unconditionally.

1927: SIGNALS
The press writes about the incredibly high milk consumption
in Zlín and the astonishing—for a beer country—lack of interest in alcohol. There is one car for every thirty-five citizens,
which is the highest rate in the whole of Czechoslovakia.

Everything is subjected to rationalization: to avoid having to summon unit managers to the phone by shouting over
the machines, a bell gives a signal in Morse code. Each unit
head has his own Morse signal, which he can hear even in
the restroom. The factory buildings have their own numbers,
too, to keep you from getting lost. All the doors in the buildings are numbered, and so are the alleyways within the factory grounds.

By crossing 21, you get to VIII/4a.

1927: HURT

There's a poster painter who works in the advertising department. When he and a colleague bring Tomáš Bata the design they've drawn, Bata stamps on the poster, without telling them what he was expecting. The second time, he leans the board against the wall at an angle and jumps right into the middle of it (once again with no explanation). The third time, he throws thirty poster designs to the floor, jumps on them, kicks the paper, and finally gives his opinion: "What kind of an idiot painted these?"

The poster painter is called Svatopluk Turek, and in a few years' time he'll start writing vindictive books about Bata.

1929: AIR

Tomáš is widening his circle of acquaintances, and his firm is now a world-famous joint-stock company. Bata's personal guest, Sir Sefton Brancker, shows the beaming Tomáš the object that will be the cause of his death.

Sir Sefton is Great Britain's director of civil aviation and has flown to Zlín to demonstrate the latest single-engine, three-seat airplane made by de Havilland. Tomáš is so impressed that he buys four on the spot.

An airport is established, and Bata's planes fly all over Europe. Soon, a factory is set up, and Zlín-brand sports airplanes go into production.

As he is flying over town, Tomáš notices a small meadow surrounded by woods. "That would make a fine graveyard," he tells the pilot.

1931: GRAPHOLOGY

Tomáš Bata's son Tomík, aged seventeen, returns from Zurich, where for the past year he has been the manager of a large store. He becomes manager of a department store in Zlín. He quarrels with his father about something. "You'll be sorry, Dad," he says, and writes a letter to Bata's biggest rival in the United States, Endicott Johnson.

He offers them his skills. Then he folds the piece of paper, but doesn't send the letter. His mother finds it and shows it to her husband, because he has instructed her to tell him everything. Tomáš triumphs: what a fabulous son he has, who can cope with anything!

On the other hand, he has an idiot for a brother. Jan Antonín, son of his father's second wife, is twenty years younger. Tomáš calls him a blockhead in front of the staff and kicks him, just like he does with the rest of his employees.

A while ago, he ordered analyses of his closest colleagues' handwriting from London graphologist Robert Saudek. He keeps them under lock and key so the victims know nothing about it. Egon Erwin Kisch will find them in the archives (in 1948 he'll start his report, *Shoe Factory*, but after writing the first page he'll die of a heart attack). Graphology Analysis #9—Jan's—reads like an arrest warrant:

1. Honesty: uncertain. If he is one of your office workers, I would not wish to cast suspicion on him on the basis of the handwriting presented to me, but I must say that I would never recommend him.
2. Initiative: greedy for short-term success, initiative of an aggressive nature. He is not a blackmailer, but he has a tendency towards it.

3. Openness: on the surface, he is frank, since he mainly comes into conflict with people. At the same time, a hypocrite.
4. Ability to make judgments: he completely misses the point.
5. Development potential: if you gave him free rein, he would be more likely to develop in a negative sense.

(In six months' time, Jan A. Bata will be given that free rein by fate. He will terrify people even more than his brother does.)

Meanwhile, Tomáš Bata must create a site for the small graveyard in the forest.

APRIL 1932: THE OPENING

"We are accustomed to regard a graveyard as a place where one comes to mourn. But, like everything in the world, a graveyard should serve life. So it should not look frightening, but like a place that the living can visit in peace and joy. Going there should be like going to a park, a place to have fun, to play, and to enjoy happy memories of the dead." With these remarks, Tomáš Bata opens the Forest Graveyard in Zlín.

(It probably doesn't occur to him that he will be the first person to be buried there.)

JULY 12, 1932, MORNING: FOG

When, at 4 a.m., he arrives at his private airfield in Otrokovice, there is a thick fog. He insists on flying. The pilot asks him to wait. "I am no friend of waiting," replies the fifty-seven-year-old Tomáš.

They take off, and seven minutes later, at a speed of ninety miles per hour, the Junkers D1608 airplane crashes into a factory chimney. The plane breaks into three parts, and a broken rib pierces Tomáš Bata's heart.

"Tomáš Bata's orders were sacred. He alone was above them. One day he gave himself an order, and died of it," writes Kisch.

HALF AN HOUR LATER: THE CHIEF
When his thirty-seven-year-old brother is informed of the disaster, he picks up the phone and calls the factory manager. "This is the Chief speaking," he introduces himself. Without batting an eyelid, he uses his brother's title, which those around him regard as blasphemy. It is said that he has taken the news of Tomáš's death as a sign from God, and has consequently started to imagine that he is the most important man on earth.

JULY 13, 1932: THE ENVELOPE
At the district court in Zlín, the envelope containing Tomáš's last will is opened. The company directors, his wife, son and brother are present. Eighteen-year-old Tomík receives cash from his father, Marie Batová receives cash and real estate. A second envelope is inscribed "FOR JAN A. BATA," and is dated a year ago. Tomáš writes that he has sold all the shares in Bata SA Zlín to Jan.

Jan opens his mouth and can't believe that for a whole year he has been the owner of Zlín and all its foreign branches! (The factory manager, one of the very few people who knew about this idea earlier, had asked Bata the reason for such a surprising decision. "The biggest scoundrel in the family will still steal less than the most honest outsider," the boss had apparently replied.)

According to the will, Jan is to manage the business at home and abroad. For quite a while he says nothing, but then he comes to his senses. Just in case, he adds to the deceased man's statement that a year ago he bought it all "under a verbal contract." By law, a verbal contract is exempt from taxes, and thus the whole thing can appear to be true—there doesn't have to be any evidence of the transaction at the tax office.

FROM 1932: A NEW ERA

Two Bata representatives fly to North Africa to investigate the potential for sales there. They send two conflicting telegrams back to Zlín. The first one says: "No one wears shoes here. No market opportunity. Am returning home."

The other one telegraphs to say: "Everyone here is barefoot. Vast market potential, send shoes as quickly as possible."

Bata shoes conquer the world, and the company acquires its own mythological status.

In the new era, statistics will be quoted constantly: in Tomáš's time, there were 24 enterprises, and in Jan's 120; in Tomáš's time, there were 1,045 stores, and in Jan's 5,810; in Tomáš's time, there were 16,560 employees, and in Jan's 105,700.

1933: SCAPEGOAT

The world crisis of the 1930s is underway. The company makes an excellent scapegoat.

In Germany, import duties on shoes go up, and it is announced that Jan Antonín Bata is a Czech Jew. Dozens of caricatures of him adorn the Nazi press: RABBI BATA SAYS IT ALL! The manager of Bata in Germany comes to Zlín to check up on the family background. They are Catholics for seven generations of cobblers; there are no documents going further back. He returns to Berlin and issues a statement to the press about Bata's origins. He is interrogated by the Gestapo. Jan decides to sell his German factory at once. In France, a factory has been in operation for a year, but it has to be closed because the competition starts up an incredible campaign: BATA IS A GERMAN. Huge photographs on the walls show Jan as the stereotypical Prussian, with fair hair and blue eyes. In Italy, the competition spreads a rumor that Bata has been attacking Mussolini in the Czechoslovak papers. In Poland, they say a secret Soviet commission visits Zlín each year: BATA HELPS THE SOVIETS.

For five years, in spite of the crisis, Czechoslovakia holds first place for the export of leather footwear worldwide.

1933: VENGEANCE—ACT ONE

The poster painter Svatopluk Turek publishes a novel called *The Shoe Machine.* The name Bata does not appear in it, but everyone is convinced it is a savage attack on "Batism."

Jan Bata sues Turek, and the court orders the destruction of all unsold copies of the novel. Two hundred gendarmerie posts conduct searches in all the bookstores in the country. (Turek claims Bata's storekeepers do what the gendarmes say because he has such a privileged position in the country.)

Plenty of periodicals defend the book. Then Bata withdraws its advertising from them; *Právo lidu*, for example, gets it back when it follows a positive review with a new, negative one.

The Shoe Machine will be reissued twenty years later when the regime changes. Then Turek will find more than eighty reports informing on him in Bata's Zlín archive. Bata was clearly trying to corner him. Later on, Turek will write that he was visited by Bata representatives who declared that if he did not give up work on his next book about Batism, he would be forced to commit suicide.

1935: BATOVKY

Jan is fascinated by numbering. For instance, the streets are called Zálešná I, Zálešná II, Zálešná III and so on up to Zálešná XII. There are more Podvesná streets than any other, seventeen in all.

Bata announces an international architectural competition for a house for the worker's family to live in. Almost three hundred architects enter. The winner is Erich Svedlund, a Swede. One house for two families. They will only have to work two hours to earn the weekly rent.

"The worker with his own home undergoes a complete transformation," Jan tells his managers.

The enlightened bourgeoisie in the West have held these views for forty years now. A small house with a garden makes a worker the actual head of a family, worthy of the name; he becomes moral and sensible, he feels tied to a place and has an influence on his relatives. At the same time it is thought that a worker who is deprived of communal accommodation, such as barracks shared with other families, will turn his back on collective demands and syndicalism.

The little houses are egalitarian and modernist. Five-yard-high (and thus small) red brick cubes, a style with no roots in tradition. People call them *batovky*, the same word they use for the shoes. On the ground floor, the family has 193 square feet for a living room, a bathroom and a kitchenette; upstairs, there is another 193 square feet for the bedroom. Thank God there are small gardens.

("It's tragic living here," Jiřina Pokorná of Bratři Sousedíků Street—wife of an electrician trained at the Bata school—will say in sixty-seven years' time. She is seventy now. "I'm going to die soon, as you can probably tell by looking at me, and all my life I've never had a proper kitchen, because this nook in the front room, sixteen square feet—that's not a kitchen, is it?"

"Why is it so small?" I ask.

"They did everything to make sure life didn't happen at home!"

In sixty-seven years, Jiřina Pokorná will be sitting outside her little red house in the garden, drinking beer quite legally.)

The houses are so close together that the residents can't help keeping an eye on each other, like it or not.

On top of that, the *batovky* on Padělky II Street are identical to the ones on Padělky IX, for example. A time-traveler from the early twenty-first century would think one and the same street was automatically reproducing itself, like in a computer game.

THE END OF 1935: THE PROPHET

"Ah, a self-duplicating town," sighs a delighted guest who visits Zlín. He is the "prophet of twentieth-century architecture," designer of some inhuman "machines for living," and his name is Le Corbusier. He was president of the jury for the competition in Zlín and Jan will ask him for a plan for the whole town too. Le Corbusier has just designed the Centrosoyuz building in Moscow, and in a few years he will be entrusted with the design for the UN building in New York.

Some time later, Jan Bata will boast to him of an idea on an even bigger scale: "I want to build copies of Zlín all over the world!"

Because of character differences, their cooperation will never come about, and the comprehensive urban planning project will be devised by two Czechs, František Gahura and Vladimír Karfík. Karfík has spent a year working for Le Corbusier, and another year working for Frank Lloyd Wright in America. Zlín will become famous as the world's first functionalist town.

LET'S GO BACK TO MAY 1935: A MONOPOLY

The social department has its spies who inform on lovers. As soon as they notice a new relationship, they report the couple. The company recommends that they get married and have children.

The manager of the personnel department, Dr. Gerbec, says: "Children are the leashes we hold their daddies by."

"Bata has a monopoly on human life," thunder the red trade unions.

"The capitalist backs all the ruling and non-ruling parties in Czechoslovakia," writes the communist newspaper, *Rudé právo*.

Indeed, in Zlín at least, there are Bata people running as candidates for all the political parties in the elections to the district council. The landowners give third place to the manager of the Bata factory in Otrokovice, the Social Democrats give a senior Bata official first place, the People's Party gives a junior Bata official third place, the nationalists give the manager of Bata's shoe finishing operations first place, and the fascists give the manager of Bata's workshops first place.

1936: NOT A STEP
This year's shoe advertisement for all of Europe: NOT A STEP WITHOUT BATA.

1936, CONTINUED: HUMANITY
An anthology of canonical texts by Jan Antonín Bata is published.

"I notice to my horror that our good old simple folk are growing up to be charity cases.

"Let us teach those among us who have lost their jobs to live modestly, but in a human way—at their own expense. By insisting that the state provide welfare for the unemployed, they are weakening the country. Let us take the work they give us, work at any price. Let us recognize that accepting hand-outs is a disgrace. Handing out welfare is not a show of humanity—it is a way to kill the human soul. It is a way of corrupting the weak."

So how is one to help those who are losing their humanity? His answer: leave them to it.

After all, those people—according to public opinion— should have died of starvation long ago, but they're still alive.

In 1931, Tomáš Bata had already warned workers who were laid off that if they accepted welfare, they would ruin any chance of ever returning to him.

The newspapers write that Zlín has no unemployment. In reality, the city evicts those who have lost their jobs from their homes and forces them to go back to their places of family origin. If anyone is a communist or is active in the unions, he won't remain in Zlín for long. Bata keeps his own private files of Reds.

In case of unrest, he has his own people—he corrupts the local policemen. For example, in January 1934, nineteen police officers from Zlín who live in Bata family homes were awarded a 60 percent rent reduction.

The communist senator Nedvěd thunders that Czechoslovak law is no longer in effect in Zlín.

Going back to the crisis—despite the fact that thousands of people have been laid off, the number of shoes produced hasn't fallen. In 1932, over a million more pairs were actually manufactured than in the previous year. "Bata-ian terror" is how the communists explain this success.

By 1936, Jan Bata has four daughters, one son and a wife

called Marie. We do not know much about his personal life, apart from the fact that two years later he will bring his wife a pair of newly invented nylon stockings from a short trip abroad. What might he say to her last thing at night?

"Our country needs our work, Maňa. We are the biggest taxpayer in our republic."

JUNE 28, 1936: LITERATURE

Jan Bata convenes a writers' conference in Zlín. Perhaps, after what happened with *The Shoe Machine*, he wants to take charge of literature.

He gives 120 men of letters a guided tour of the town, and then lets them take the floor.

"I feel great joy at seeing industry and literature together. These two elements should be united," declares a former author of decadent fiction, Karel Scheinpflug, on behalf of the writers of Prague, and adds: "Literature can do a lot for industry, and vice versa."

Bata tells the writers about his own cultural needs and those of the citizens of Zlín. "Our fight to improve people has been a success."

NEXT DAY: SURREALISM

The 120 writers view the work of 152 painters at the Jan Bata Art Salon. (Four months earlier, Bata had organized an artists' conference.) He casts a tolerant eye upon the works of the greatest artists, which he has bought. His gaze comes to a stop

GOTTLAND   31

on a painting by Toyen (known earlier as Marie Čermínová), who paints eggs, stones and string to illustrate delusions; her work was highly praised by Paul Eluard when he visited Prague.

"I admit," says Jan Antonín Bata, "that I try to find people who haven't got lost in a single style. I know of a young fellow who paints dead chicks. Or men who look as if they only have an hour to live. I don't think that's right. Whom do these crude daubs serve? Society? The social classes? The nation? There's one picture in particular I can't get out of my mind: Slovaks with axes, and sparks flying from their eyes, who appear to be moving forwards—give me a break! I want to help artists. But only the kind who paint human beings, the kind who want something."

(Despite Bata's narrow views about art, the next four Salons that he organized did enliven the artistic environment; the shows were viewed by 300,000 people.)

"Aha," says Jan, remembering that he is talking to writers, not painters, "you too should avoid pessimism. And get on with drawing up a credo for the working people."

1937: THE ELEVATOR

Jan is probably feeling handsome and desirable: the construction of two academic institutes is nearly over, and work on what will be the tallest skyscraper in the republic is just starting. It is to have sixteen floors and will be 254 feet high. It will be Bata's office block.

Another eleven years will go by before the British writer

George Orwell publishes the principles of life under the watchful eye of Big Brother, but Jan is ahead of world literature. He comes up with the idea of creating something that has never existed before: his own mobile office space which follows his employees about the building. He situates it in a glazed elevator which moves up and down the tower block. This cabin is 16 x 16 feet, and has a sink with hot running water, a radio and air conditioning.

He doesn't have to leave the elevator, nor does he have to take the stairs. For instance, his office stops on the thirteenth floor, the wall of the building moves aside and from his mobile throne room, Jan Antonín Bata can see the people at work.

He says it's for their good too: they don't have to give up a lot of time to come see the Chief.

If the need should arise, his office can appear on another floor in moments.

CIRCA 1937, CONTINUED: THE BEST

Jan Bata founds a "School for the Best," drawn from the School for Young Men. At mealtimes, the students can only speak in foreign languages, and the tables are set as they are in five-star hotels (Jan has just come back from a two-month journey around the world). They study in tuxedos, and remove their top hats only when they cross the school's threshold.

On the other hand, after classes they dress in ordinary laborer's clothes and go to work.

Despite Jan's successes, old Mrs. Batová (meaning the late Tomáš's wife, who is not old, but people call her that to

distinguish her from Jan's wife, who is also called Marie Batová) never stops referring to him as "that cretin."

Jan, who only completed elementary school, receives an
honorary doctorate from the Higher Technical School in
Brno and insists on being called "Professor."

MARCH 12, 1938: PATAGONIA

He talks too much. Caution is the mother of wisdom—so
said the Good Soldier Švejk*—but like Švejk himself, Jan Bata
never abides by this saying.

The day after Austria is incorporated into the Third Reich,
sensing the fate that is to befall Czechoslovakia in the near
future, he wakes up with an idea. In a short while from now,
the imminent power struggle will begin. Even Warsaw regards Czechoslovakia as an artificial creation, doomed to
destruction.

In his own newspaper, *Zlín*, Jan Antonín Bata publicizes
his idea—to move Czechoslovakia to South America.

"Brazil is as large as the whole of Europe and has forty-
four million citizens, while Europe has four hundred and
eighty million. Why seek land for development in cramped
Europe? Why not there instead? Better to move out. The last
war cost the world eight trillion Czech crowns. Transferring
ten million people to South America would only cost fourteen
billion crowns. And for one hundred and forty billion they
could build themselves beautiful farms. Why do something

---

* Švejk is the eponymous hero of the classic Czech satirical novel by Jaroslav
Hašek about the absurd adventures of an incompetent soldier serving in the
army of the Austro-Hungarian Empire during the First World War.

so stupid and harmful to people as to have a war? Patagonia in southern Argentina would also be highly suitable for us."

Bata is counting on the Germans liking this idea. They'd be relieved if the Czechs were to move out. (During his trial after the war, in communist Czechoslovakia, this will be the pretext for accusing him of betraying the nation.)

"But a nation and its culture are closely tied to one place," he hears from all quarters.

"To hell with culture if children have to die in a war," he replies.

1938 OR 1939: GÖRING

He has a private meeting in Berlin with Reichsmarschall Hermann Göring. The communists will write that he did it immediately after the Germans first occupied Czechoslovakia—thus, in March 1939. Jan's family will say it was half a year earlier, in the fall. The communists will say it was his own idea to make personal contact with Göring. The family will say he was forced to do it—a courier arrived from Berlin and threatened consequences if Bata did not appear before him. Even Tomík, who wasn't fond of his uncle, will have an explanation for his intentions: "He was only pushed towards Göring by curiosity and a sense of his own importance."

I couldn't find any reliable evidence on what the two men talked about. Apart from the fact that, in his book *The Treachery of the Bata Family*, the former poster painter from the advertising department quotes Jan as saying: "Göring told me in person that we are living in Germany's backyard, that we must take that fact on board and act accordingly. Of course, there's a lot of truth in that."

In any case, all exports will now be marked "Made in Germany." The footwear is for the Wehrmacht, but no firm under occupation has any alternative. Hitler will even arrange for arms industry experts to become familiar with the working system at Zlín. "Of all the Slavs, the Czech is the most dangerous, because he is diligent," says Hitler.

During the war, the firm increases its number of workers fourfold.

Jan Bata informs them that from now on freedom can only flourish with the help of enterprise. But he himself leaves for America immediately.

JULY 1939: CYCLIST

Of course, he has to tell the Germans that he's going to the World's Fair in New York, otherwise they wouldn't let him leave the Protectorate of Bohemia and Moravia. But he knows he will remain in the United States. Meanwhile, twenty-five-year-old Tomík and his mother are in Canada. Tomík was on a trip when the Germans invaded Bohemia. He has decided not to go back.

The Germans try to take over Zlín and the surrounding area. The law of the Protectorate allows them to confiscate property if the owner is abroad.

However, Jan Bata has protected himself: he has given 7 percent of his shares apiece to each of the five members of the supervisory board. Now he encourages the older Mrs. Batová to return to Zlín, because she owns 25 percent of the shares. She goes back to prevent Zlín from passing into foreign hands. In America, Jan has only 40 percent of the remaining shares, and thus the majority of Bata's owners are living in occupied territory. Of course, Jan has declarations in writing stored in a New York bank vault, stating that when the war is over the members of the supervisory board will return his shares to him.

Apparently, this makes Hitler fly into a rage. "The Czechs are like cyclists—they hunch their upper bodies, but pedal below!" he screams.

JANUARY 1941: GREAT STREAM
Jan and his family leave Los Angeles on the SS *America*.

He is an undesirable visitor in the United States, where he has ended up on the Allies' blacklist as a collaborator whose enterprise works for the Germans. He sails for Brazil.

Twenty-seven-year-old Tomík is still in Canada and starts to manage a duplicate of Zlín called Batawa.

In Brazil, Jan founds his own duplicates. He asks the Indians what water is called. "Y," they reply.

"And how do you say good?"

"Pora," they politely inform him. And thus duplicate number one is born, the small town of Bataypora.

Duplicate number two is called Bataguassu, which means "Bata Great Stream."

JUNE 1942: A DISPLAY
Since 1929, there has been a department store on Wenceslas Square in Prague called the Bata Palace, with a large display window. (It was designed by a Czech named Ludvík Kysela,

and in the twenty-first century it will be regarded as one of the most remarkable functionalist buildings in the world.)

On May 27, 1942, a group of Czechoslovak paratroopers trained in Britain makes an attempt on the life of Reinhard Heydrich, the most important official of the Third Reich in the Protectorate, who dies in the hospital. The attackers manage to escape. As punishment, Hitler orders the entire village of Lidice, near Prague, exterminated.* Not only do the Nazis kill all the men, send the women to Ravensbrück and take the children to another camp or to Germany, not only do they burn down or blow up all the buildings and raze the village to the ground, but they also go under the ground—they drag the coffins out of the graves and remove the corpses. The operation is considered complete once all the trees have been uprooted and the stream bed has been diverted, so that no one can tell there was ever a village there at all.

Before the Germans catch the assassins, the authorities force the manager of the Bata store on Wenceslas Square to display in the window an overcoat, hat, briefcase and bicycle found at the site of the attack and an announcement offering a reward of ten million crowns for finding the assailants.

(For communist propaganda, the display in the window will later be part of the evidence that Bata collaborated with the occupying forces.)

---

* Afterwards, a village called Ležáky would also be destroyed, where the telegraph operator from the group was hiding.

1945: FAME AND INFAMY

First, Zlín is bombed by the Americans (they destroy 60 percent of the town's factories), and then it is liberated by the
Red Army. The Polish government-in-exile refuses to reach a
compromise with the USSR and remains in London forever.
The Czechoslovak government-in-exile creates a coalition
government with the communists in Moscow and announces
its own program.

The directors of the Bata plants are arrested. Their deputies are forced to sweep the streets of Zlín publicly. In the
course of two months, 13,000 inhabitants flee from the town
of 50,000.

Ivan H. and Josef V. make a speech from the factory
broadcasting center. During the war, they worked for the firm
and were informers for the Gestapo. Now they have signed up
with the Security Service—the secret police. "Jan Bata's fame
has ended in infamy," they say.

Jan is living in Batatuba (duplicate number three in Brazil), where he finds out that by decree of the president of the
republic the state has taken over the joint-stock company of
Bata A.S.

The famous Soviet writer Ilya Ehrenburg visits Czechoslovakia, and writes: "Bata, who remained in Zlín, praised the
Führer and supplied the Reichswehr with footwear. On the
eve of Munich, he changed his coat of arms. Until then, it was
three shoes, but Bata painted in a fourth, so that the crossed
lines would form a swastika."

Did Ehrenburg really go to Zlín? (After all, Bata had left
the country and had no coat of arms.) This quotation from his

article is distributed all over Czechoslovakia, and the communists prepare a lawsuit against Jan Bata, who is charged with betraying the nation.

Meanwhile, he demands compensation from the Czechoslovak state for the nationalized town of Zlín—the greatest fortune owned by a single man in Central Europe.

If the court can prove that he collaborated with the Germans, he isn't owed a thing.

APRIL 28, 1947: THE VERDICT

"My God, we created Zlín purely in order to give the Czechs wings," says Jan Bata when he finds out that the national court in Prague has sentenced him to fifteen years in prison and ten years' forced labor. And has confiscated his property.

He demanded to be allowed to appear before the court and to be given a chance to defend himself. "I do not believe the accused would really want to appear in court," said the chairman of the prosecution team during the trial.

So the prosecutor declared: "An indictment can take place in the absence of an accused man who refuses to come to the country and will not be coming."

The accused asked at least to be sent the bill of indictment. To no effect.

Although the trial was a typical Stalinist show-trial, it failed to prove collaboration by means of production: all factory owners were forced to manufacture for the Germans, and he had not even been in the country. It also failed to recognize the comical idea involving Patagonia as treason.

However, the court did reach the conclusion that failing to support the underground resistance movement in Bohemia was a form of collaboration.

The Brazilian authorities quickly exchange Bata's permanent residency card for citizenship, thanks to which they can protest: their citizen has not been tried according to international procedure. This is to no avail.

Forty-five years from now, one of Jan's grandsons will conduct a private investigation in order to rehabilitate his grandfather. In 1992, a report will be found in an FBI archive recording that the Americans had wanted to cross the name Bata off their blacklist, as there was no proof of collaboration. However, the communist authorities in Prague did all they could to keep the name on the list, because otherwise it would have been impossible to prosecute him in Czechoslovakia or to confiscate his property.

1949: SVIT

In honor of Comrade Klement Gottwald, a faithful disciple of Stalin, who a year earlier had led the total takeover of power by the communists and announced: "With the Soviet Union forever and ever, never otherwise," Zlín is renamed Gottwaldov. Bata shoes are renamed Svit (meaning "dawn") shoes.

1949: IVANA

In what is now Gottwaldov, a daughter, Ivana, is born to a worker at the plant, a Mr. Zelníčkov. Twenty years from now she will become a model, and after that, Ivana Trump, wife of the billionaire Donald Trump and one of the richest women in the United States. She will live in a fifty-room apartment in the sixty-eight-story Trump Tower in New York, famous for its rococo interior.

The American press will call her "the spiritual heiress of the capitalist genius from Zlín who injected an Anglo-Saxon mentality into a Slav body."

The couple will divorce because—as her husband will claim—his biggest mistake was to let a Czech woman from Zlín join the company. Instead of a wife, he got an indefatigable business partner.

One of the most interesting thoughts expressed in the bestseller that Ivana T. will write about herself fifty years later is this: "A woman is like a tea bag. You never know how strong she is until she gets into hot water."

1957: NOBEL

For years now, everyone in Prague has been saying: "With the Soviet Union forever, and not a moment longer!"

They also say that Bata will get the Nobel Prize—so rumor has it.

In fact, the Brazilian press writes that sixty-year-old Jan Bata is a candidate for the Nobel Peace Prize for his plan to relocate Czechoslovakia to Patagonia, in other words, the modern concept of migration. The Brazilian president has put his name forward for the prize—for invaluable services in changing the world. (However, the prize is awarded to Canadian politician Lester B. Pearson for solving the Suez crisis.)

Goethe said: "More light!" and then died. Beethoven's last

words were: "The comedy is over," and Heine's were: "God will forgive me—that's his profession."

What might the last words of a Nobel-prizewinning Jan Antonín Bata have been?

"MY SHOES DO NOT CHAFE THE FEET"?

1957: AN EXPERIMENT

According to the press, Jan Bata initiated an experiment in Brazil to find ways of increasing the surface area of a cow's hide.

He gave the following instructions: "We will put horsefly larvae in small openings all over the cow's skin. They will cause blisters, the skin will stretch, and as a result its surface area will increase by 60 percent."

The experiment was suspended after the death of the first cow.

Bata's next experiment, involving a wooden railroad, was halted when the wooden rails came apart under the first cast-iron locomotive.

Of course, this has no connection with the fact that Bata's shoes are still selling like hot cakes.

THE 1950S AND '60S: WAR

Now Jan Bata is at war with Marie Batová and her son Tomík. Wherever there are Bata branches and organizations (in over thirty countries), his sister-in-law and nephew accuse him of illegally seizing property left by Tomáš Bata. Their fight is described by the entire Western press. As a result of the legal and media intrigue, Jan is even arrested in New York for two weeks.

He is worn out. He is in bad health and has no money. The court cases go on for fifteen years. Finally, in 1962, Jan Bata renounces a large part of his property in favor of Marie and Tomík. He dies in 1965 in São Paulo.

The Canadian Bata (Tomík's branch) takes over worldwide command from the Brazilian Bata. In several dozen countries there are several different Bata companies in operation; for example, in France alone there are eight, each of which has daughter companies that it controls. Tomík's son Thomas Bata supervises the entire organization.

For its own purposes, the Bata Shoe Organization publishes a journal called *The Peak*.

1959: VENGEANCE—THE NEXT ACT

The poster painter has already committed several acts of vengeance. He has re-issued *The Shoe Machine*, and published *The Treachery of the Bata Family* and also *Bataism Abridged*. Now he brings out *The True Face of Bataism*, in which he has collected the accounts of former Bata employees.

"I worked in building No. 31. The foreman called us rude names, unrepeatable names. When I received a telegram saying that my little daughter had died, I asked the foreman for some time off to go the funeral. 'What would you do there? There's fuck all you can do—you're hardly going to bring the child back to life. Get lost—nobody's going to meet the production target for you.' I don't know how I got back to the machine because I couldn't see through my tears. Despite his threats, I went to the funeral. What I then suffered for the next three years is impossible to relate" (A. Wagner).

"Bata approached our parents, asking them to sell him their beloved orchard. They refused, because they'd waited twenty years for it to produce fruit. My brother, my sister, and I were already supporting ourselves—we were all working for Bata. The head of personnel threatened us, saying that if we didn't force our parents to sell the land, we needn't bother coming to work the next day. So we put pressure on our poor father, who wept as he sold the land for a fifth of its value, just because Mr. Bata had a whim" (Josef and František Hradil).

In analyzing the documents, the author reveals that in the period from 1927 to 1937 not a single worker went from Bata into retirement. The workforce was systematically rejuvenated. Workers were laid off for any reason at all at least ten years before retirement.

"This was how the era broke people, this was how the old regime debased them," adds Turek.

1959, CONTINUED: MOSCOW
Another author (who probably bears no grudge, but is a historian) points out how, at the linguistic level, refined Bataism is now blurring class divisions and tempering the system of exploitation.

He writes that Bata cunningly calls its employees "co-workers," and their wages are "a share of the profits."

On the tenth anniversary of the establishment of Gottwaldov and Svit, the press quotes the words of a certain communist who, as early as 1932, told Bata: "Moscow is do-ing away with human envy, while Bata uses envy as a driv-ing force."

MARCH 1990: THE RETURN
Gottwaldov is called Zlín again.

Sixty years on, Tomáš Bata (Tomík) arrives triumphantly in the city. He is greeted by 100,000 people.

"Come and oppress us, Bata!" they shout.

He visits his former stores. In one of them, he sees a cus-tomer trying on some shoes. "My customers are my life," he says. "I'm upset when the buyers have to do up their own shoelaces in one of my stores." He gets down on his knees and starts tying the man's shoelaces for him.

LUCERNA PALACE

It's 1906.

Vácslav Havel, a Czech engineer from Prague, is planning to build a latter-day palace downtown, on Wenceslas Square. It will be the first building in Prague to be made out of reinforced concrete. He shows his wife the design. "What a lot of windows," says his wife. "It'll look like a lantern."

The Czech word for "lantern" is *lucerna*.

"And that's an excellent name for the entire building!" says her husband excitedly. "But best of all," he adds, "it's a Czech word which any foreigner can pronounce easily."

JUST A WOMAN

"I was just a woman," she said.

"In the end, she's just a woman," said those who loved her.

We don't know what she said as she was dying. We do know what her best friend revealed on her own deathbed.

"After cremation, I don't want a funeral or any sort of ceremony," said her friend.

"Where are your ashes to be scattered?" asked the notary recording her will.

"Nowhere!" she replied. "I don't want to spoil the flowers in someone's garden."

She sat in her bedroom in Salzburg (538 square feet), watching videos of herself in leading roles, and waiting.

In 1995, as she sat on the sofa in calm anticipation, Helena Třeštíková from Prague asked her: "What is your greatest wish, Miss Baarová?"

"The only thing I'm looking forward to is death," she replied.

Unfortunately, death did not come for her until five years later.

First, she was cremated at Europe's biggest crematorium.

Then the urn was placed in the family grave. She was laid on top of her mother (who had lain there for fifty-five years), her sister (who had been lying on top of their mother for fifty-four years), and her father (who had been lying on top of the two of them for thirty-five years).

Her mother had been killed by a heart attack at the very moment she was asked about Lída's jewelry.

Her sister killed herself, when she was refused admission to her favorite theater because of Lída.

Her father died of cancer. Lída had nothing directly to do with his death. But even so he suffered: he hadn't seen her for seventeen years, and never did, to the day he died. The state had deprived him of the right to see his daughter in perpetuity.

She was already a student at drama school when a movie director saw her and invited her to the studio. That was when her father, Karel Babka, head of the municipal council in Prague, came up with the idea that she would be called Lída Baarová. Ludmila Babková sounded too ordinary for an artist. Her father didn't think long about what her name should be, because he had a writer friend called Jindřich Šimon Baar.

Her old first name didn't suit her new surname.

In those days, in neighboring Germany, a man was gaining absolute power who—as somebody once noted—was most grateful to his father for dropping the common, rustic surname Schicklgruber.

It goes without saying. The greeting "Heil Schicklgruber" would have been too lengthy.

They made a movie, but the director realized that he should entrust seventeen-year-old Lída Baarová to better hands. He took her to see a younger colleague. It was 1931, and for two years the Bio Lucerna, the country's first movie theater with sound, had been up and running in Prague. "When it comes to the talkies, I'm helpless," the director confided to his colleague. "In the silent pictures, everything was simpler. When I didn't know how to shoot a particular scene, I added a caption to say what the actress was thinking at that moment, and the audience could read it themselves."

The younger colleague (the director Otakar Vávra, who was born in 1911 and died in 2011) took Lída on and directed her best Czech movies. He always used to say (well, perhaps not always, but in the 1990s, as he couldn't have said it earlier) that she quickly became a star of a kind that the Czechs still don't have, to this day. "Compared with Baarová, today's actresses look like slatterns," he wrote.

In the late 1930s, one of her fans named a new variety of rose after her. The flower had dark red petals in the middle, and delicate pink ones on the outside.

As someone wrote of her: "She knows how to act sincerely—hers is a face which only shows pure emotions."

At a theater premiere in Prague she was spotted by the head of the German studio UFA, which the Germans regarded as

Europe's equivalent of Hollywood. It was September 1934, and Lída was sitting in the auditorium with her mother.

From the next day on she was only allowed to eat three apples a day, and nothing else. "She has to slim down at any cost to get rid of her Slavic chubbiness," the producer kept saying.

The movie was called *Barcarole*. They were looking for an actress to play the most beautiful woman in Venice. "I was twenty, and I was in heaven," she said. "The leading role in a German movie. No Czech actress had ever achieved that before."

There was one topic on which Lída said one thing to her friends, something else to the American investigators, something quite different to the Czechoslovak Security Service and something else again to the reporter who wrote a book about her called *The Curse of Lída Baarová*.

The way she spoke about this topic when she was drinking water was quite different from the way she spoke about it when drinking copious amounts of champagne mixed with Fernet.

The topic was love.

From here on, most of what we know about Baarová should be labeled with the first sentence from Kurt Vonnegut's *Slaughterhouse-Five*, which goes: "All this happened, more or less."

• • •

One day during filming, the gondolas on the artificial canals suddenly stopped moving. She saw the face of her co-star Gustav Fröhlich—who for some days now had been her lover—take on a new, radiant expression.*

"The Führer is coming!" everyone kept saying excitedly.

She wanted to hide, but Hitler's eyes came to rest on her.

"His eyes were blue-gray," she later explained at her interrogation. "Eyes like the coldest steel. He was staring at me insistently, as if he were literally boring into me with those eyes of his."

He squeezed her hand tightly. The visit only lasted a short while.

Three days later, Lída received word that Hitler was inviting her to the Reich Chancellery for tea. Gustav and the director said she had to go. She was so frightened that she had an attack of diarrhea. Some people were saying that thanks to the Führer there was no unemployment, and that he would defend Germany against the Bolsheviks, while others said he was a monster.

"What a lovely little hat you have," said Hitler.

There was a fire in the grate.

"Would you like to be German?"

"I am Czech. Does it bother you?"

"No. But I'd be pleased if you were German."

Hitler's secretary left the room, and they were alone.

"When I saw you at the studio," he began, "I was stunned.

---

* Gustav Fröhlich played the lead in Fritz Lang's legendary 1926 movie *Metropolis*.

Your face reminds me of a woman who played an important role in my life. Suddenly she was alive before me."

She didn't know whom she resembled.

Only later did she hear the story of Geli—Angela Raubal, Hitler's niece from Vienna, with whom he fell hopelessly in love as soon as she reached the age of sixteen. Geli had nothing in common with the Nordic race: like Lída, she had dark eyes, black hair and high cheekbones. She was found dead on the carpet in his apartment in Munich. She had shot herself through the heart for reasons which were never explained.

Hitler felt responsible for Geli, so, since her death in 1931, to atone for his spiritual part in her suicide, he had stopped eating meat.

"The photograph that stands always on my desk came to life," he told Lída in 1934. "That is to your credit."

"I'm extremely sorry . . ." she replied helplessly.

He said nothing more and allowed her to leave.

As we all know, each item that is processed by the memory becomes something completely new. Stress releases chemical compounds in the brain, which immediately impoverish our future memories. Moreover, after the war Lída could have told lies on purpose.

Thus we don't know how many times she actually had tea with Hitler. In her diary, she wrote that she went twice, but towards the end of her life she maintained she only went once.

However, she told the Security Service that she went
four times.

The second man to favor her with a penetrating, lingering
gaze had one leg shorter than the other.

His shorter, right leg was twisted to the inside, and his
right knee was one and a half inches smaller in circumference
than the left.

His long hands did not fit his short arms.

He was a slight figure, the height of a boy.

All through his childhood, the other children had teased
him, and his father had ignored him.

He had sexual intercourse for the first time at the age of
thirty-three.

He enrolled at five different universities.

He only went to a Nazi Party meeting to keep warm, because he had no winter overcoat.

The first time he saw Hitler, he wrote: "Those large blue
eyes of his! Like stars! He is pleased to see me!"

The first time Lída Baarová saw this man, she was struck
by how unattractive he was.

It was said that his brilliant intelligence made him doubly
unlikeable.

The most famous idea that he engendered, "If you repeat
a lie often enough it becomes the truth," had long since been
put into action.

Publishing photographs in which his shorter leg was visible carried the risk of death. According to a writer who had
a private meeting with him during the war, "the Minister of

Propaganda was surrounded by a demonic aura: anyone who came close to him felt the sort of fear that accompanies a man crossing a high-voltage zone."

Then Lída Baarová heard his voice. "I felt as if it had entirely pervaded me. As if it were warming and stroking me all at once," she said.

She met Goebbels by accident in the street. He invited her to come and see what a lovely house he had and what beautiful children. He boasted that all of them had names beginning with H, in honor of Hitler.

Then he kept inviting her and Gustav to parties and premieres. Whenever they were ready to leave, it would turn out that the minister had a movie at home containing something he didn't like, and he wanted Lída and Gustav to see it before the premiere. They were actors. They couldn't refuse the minister who was personally in charge of cinema. Just like the Führer, he believed the radio, the automobile and the cinema would help the Reich to ultimate victory. After the war, historians worked out that the minister had had sexual relations with thirty-six performers of lead and supporting roles.

Finally, he invited her to his office for tea on her own.

He asked what her husband was filming today.

She replied that she didn't have a husband, and Goebbels got a shock.

When the Czechs arrested her after the war, she refused to acknowledge having been his guest at a Nazi rally in Nuremberg.

Two days after her twenty-second birthday (September 9,

1936), following a reception that evening, Goebbels asked her to go with him to the hotel where Hitler was staying. In the restaurant they heard someone singing: "I am so very much in love . . ."

"So am I," he whispered in her ear.

In reply she told him how unhappy she was with Gustav, who was refusing to marry her. He would appear with her in public, but only to draw attention to himself. He would put jewelry on her before going out, but when they arrived home he would immediately take it off her, so that nothing would happen to it. On top of that, at night he'd get confused and call her by another woman's name.

"Please stay until tomorrow," said Goebbels. "At noon I have an important speech to make—please watch me closely as I do so."

He took a handkerchief from his breast pocket. "I shall touch it to my lips as a sign that I am thinking about you."

Lída kissed him tenderly on the cheek.

"The Jew is a parasite! A destroyer of culture! An enzyme of decay!" he said the next day, and reached for his handkerchief.

She was shooting a movie version of *Die Fledermaus* for the UFA studio when the Austrian actress playing the role of Adela was banned from performing. The director asked Lída to intercede with Goebbels. The ban was withdrawn, and the crew were full of admiration for Baarová, but the gutter press described her as "the Herr Minister's new girlfriend."

"You see," he then said. "People are convinced we are intimate, but you keep running away from it."

He tried to embrace her; as usual at such moments, she
burst into tears.

"But you have children, and I have Gustav . . ."

"No, you don't, you can drop that idea. A beautiful woman
is like a yacht on the open sea. Every gust of wind drives her
in one direction or another—when the gale passes, there's
always a fine storm waiting for her."

"So if a woman is born beautiful, her beauty is a sin?"

"Not a sin, but an inconvenience. A beautiful woman is
tossed about like a reed."

"Whenever he phoned me at home he always introduced himself as Herr Müller. From day to day, 'Herr Müller' sounded
more and more like an order."

"He calls her so often that Göring has had to hire an extra
employee to tap her phone."

Richard Walther Darré, the pig-farming expert appointed
Nazi minister of health, explained that women's aspirations to
be emancipated were due to a malfunction of the sex glands.
He regarded woman as a daydreaming, ruminative domestic animal. The most desirable female characteristics were
defined by a typical advertisement which read: "Fifty-two-
year-old doctor, Aryan, wishing to settle in the countryside,
desires male offspring in an official relationship with a healthy
Aryan woman, a virgin, young, modest and frugal, capable of
hard work, wide-hipped, who walks on flat heels and does not
wear earrings, ideally of limited means." Goebbels explained

that the Nazis were removing women from public life in order to restore their dignity to them.

When he invited Lída to the rally, Magda Goebbels—the
Third Reich's ideal woman—was thirty-five, and pregnant
with her fifth child; after the fourth she had gained weight.
She was still attractive. She was patron of the National Institute of Fashion, and proudly wore an Order of Motherhood.

The authors of an American publication, *Three in Love*,
in a chapter entitled "Ménage and the Holocaust," note that:
"Goebbels wished to move his mistress in with his wife and
children. The Aryan for progeny, the Slav (or Jew) for illicit
passion—such was the inherent contradiction of the Nazi's
erotic world."

On August 3, 1937, Goebbels wrote in his personal diary: "Bohemia is not a state," and as Lída had agreed to come to the
rally in Nuremberg, he noted that "a miracle has occurred."

On October 19, 1937, he wrote: "This state-for-a-season
must disappear!" Sometime later, he added that when the first
mild frost came he and Lída had been to the forest to feed
the deer.

On March 20, 1938, he noted: "All the Jews and Czechs
must be quickly expelled from Vienna"; at the same time he
was teaching her archery, and he was singing.

On June 1, 1938, he quoted Hitler: "I am staying with the
Führer. He characterizes the Czechs as brash, deceitful, and
servile. By mobilizing their army they are placing a noose
around their own necks. Now they are living only on fear." He
played the piano for Lída.

A few days later, Magda Goebbels, who was twelve years older than Baarová, invited her to come and see her.

She greeted her in a friendly way. According to Lída, in an over-friendly way. "I love my husband, but he is in love with you," she said.

"I would like to leave Germany. Could you help me?" asked Lída.

"Let's be on informal terms," said Magda, pouring liqueur from a carafe and raising her glass to clink it against Lída's. "You can't do that. He is a great man. He needs you as well as me."

"I could never . . ."

"You'll have to."

The wife of Martin Bormann, head of the surveillance service—who had nine children with her and was in love with an actress called Manja Behrens—wrote about her husband's lover: "M. is so nice that I can't be angry. All the children adore her. She is even a better housewife than I am. She helped me to pack the china dinner service. Not a single saucer was broken."

Lída Baarová spent four weekends with the Goebbels family at their summer home on the Wannsee.

After the final weekend, "Herr Müller" called her and uttered just two sentences: "My wife has gone to see the Führer. She is a devil."

Hitler summoned Goebbels and forbade him to communicate with Baarová. "I'll get divorced," announced the minister. "I can become ambassador to Japan and live there with her."

"That is not what the nation wants!" said Hitler, thumping his fist against the desk. "He who creates history has no right to a personal life."

"The Führer behaved like a father," Goebbels wrote in his diary. "I am grateful to him for that. Right now that's just what I need. I have spent an hour in the car, driving a long way and to no purpose. Then I have one more long, sad phone call to make. I shall be tough, although my heart is breaking."

"He wept!" wrote Lída. "He wept like an ordinary person."

When he called to tell her it was over because he had given the Führer his word, she lost consciousness.

The next day she was taken to a mental hospital.

When she came out she was summoned by the police. "You are banned from performing in the movies or on stage," she heard. "You cannot appear in public."

She fainted. After that, the only thing that could calm her down was a shot of morphine.

She stopped receiving letters.

A ban was imposed on showing any of the movies she had made for the UFA studio.

She took only cash and her handbag.

In Prague, she stood outside a house that was unfamiliar to her. It had been her parents' job to spend her wages on

a house, and they had bought a fantastic modernist villa—
it resembled a ship, with a surrounding terrace that looked
like a deck. There were no right angles; the kitchen was semi-
circular and the bedroom circular. The windows were round.
Outside the house grew roses of the Lída variety.

Her sister was cold towards her. "Do you know what we've
been through?" she asked. "Do you know what the Germans
did to us?"

Seven years younger, her sister Zorka Babková—with the
new surname Janů—was also an actress.

By "us" she meant the country.

When, as a result of the betrayal by Britain and France,
Czech Sudetenland was suddenly occupied by Germany in
fall 1938, Jews, Czechs and anti-fascist Germans fled from
there deep into Bohemia. Those who ran away too late were
arrested by the Nazis. Those who managed to escape earlier
were left with no home, no food and no chance of employment. Agencies were set up which specialized in rapidly send-
ing the refugees who had ended up in Prague abroad ("I can
send doctors, lawyers, and Israelite tradesmen to the other
hemisphere immediately. I have a permit.")

"Even the soldiers cried. Lída, do you know how unhappy
people are who have to run away?"

Lída didn't know.

"I'm very sorry," she replied helplessly. "I had so many
problems of my own," she added, "that I could no longer picture your situation."

●　●　●

The question which, during her conversations with Lída Baarová shortly before her death, had interested Helena Třeštíková, a filmmaker from Czech Television, and Stanislav Motl, a journalist for the TV Nova television station, as well as dozens of people who had once known her and, since the 1990s, were willing to talk about it, was this: was Lída Baarová stupid?

She herself claimed that she was.

But she was the last person to be believed. For her that could have been a very convenient answer.

On the night of March 14 to 15, 1939, Hitler forced Czechoslovakia to capitulate. He demanded that President Emil Hácha come to Berlin, and threatened to bomb Prague if the Czechs did not submit. The country had been carved up after Munich, had no border defenses to the north and no chance of resistance. Early in the morning, before Hácha got back from Berlin (his train was held up at the border for a long time, supposedly because of a snowstorm), Hitler was already at the castle in Prague. From the start, it was clear that the Czechs wouldn't defend themselves. Their closest friends, France and Great Britain, were siding with Hitler, so now they had two options: to follow the example of Jan Hus, thirteenth-century priest and martyr—save face and go up in flames—or capitulate and survive.

At 8:15 a.m., the German army was driving down Prague's National Avenue.

There were crowds walking along the streets, but nobody stopped, nobody looked around. On Old Town Square, at the

Tomb of the Unknown Soldier, people were laying piles of snowdrops and weeping.

There was no fear in the air, no sounds of lament or despair. There was just sorrow.

"Each one of us took a major task upon himself on the fifteenth of March," the reporter Milena Jesenská wrote a few days later in the weekly *Přítomnost*.

The task was this: to be Czech.

"The only gesture which Czech men could have made on the fifteenth of March 1939 would have been a suicidal one. It may be a beautiful thing to shed blood for your homeland. I don't even think it's particularly hard to do that. But we must do something very different. We must live. We must save every person we have, every bit of strength, great and small. There are not enough of us to allow ourselves to make gestures. There are only eight million of us here—too few, far too few for suicide. But quite enough for life."

And so the task was to work as usual, and whenever possible, to cheat the regime. Above all, not to become German.

Before noon, Lída Baarová was also driving down National Avenue. Even though she had been back in Prague for two-and-a-half months by now, she hadn't yet removed the German license plates from her car. As soon as she stopped the vehicle, the passers-by took one look at the plates and thumped their fists on the roof in anger.

The summer of 1939 was not yet over. Lída went to a soccer match with the singer Ljuba Hermanová. By now everyone was talking about war. "But a while earlier Lída had started to speak Czech badly," recalled her friend. "She was always mixing up Czech and German words. That day we were sitting in the stands, when she suddenly started shouting in an affected way: 'Herrgott, now they could shoot a ... *wie sagt man das auf tschechisch?* ... yes, a goal!' That should have given us, her friends, a clue. At least about how stupid she was. I can't imagine anyone in the least bit intelligent destroying her own life to that extent."

At a later point, the director Otakar Vávra remembered her in Prague using a powder compact with a photo of Goebbels on it, though naturally he bore no grudge against her. She was just a woman. She lost her head. She was in love. She forgot her principles.

Czech society was supposed to work solely for the benefit of the Third Reich.

"How do you explain why so many Czechs come in here and greet us with 'Heil Hitler'?" a German asked Milena Jesenská.

"Czechs? You must be mistaken."

"No, I'm not. They come into our office, stretch out their right hand, and say: 'Heil Hitler.' Why is that? I could also tell you about a writer who makes a persistent effort to have his plays performed on the Berlin stage as soon as possible. I could tell you about all sorts of people who do far more than they have to—eagerly and tirelessly."

Perhaps Baarová wasn't stupid, but just wanted to make life comfortable for herself? Perhaps because she believed that Hitler was bound to have the final word in Europe?

"No, no. She was just a young woman, that's the only explanation," said her defenders years later.

According to Stanislav Motl, the journalist who wrote a book about her: "As a star, she felt she was exempt from thinking about important things."

Later on, people kept saying that on March 15 Lída Baarová had welcomed Hitler at the castle in Prague—this is not true.

In November 1942, when Goebbels came to Prague for a three-day visit, Lída was forbidden to leave the city for the duration—this is true.

At the Lucerna Palace, where the movie world used to meet in the bar, she was boycotted, and there were lots of people who refused to sit next to her—this is partly true.

She did have some good friends. She was helped by Miloš Havel, uncle of the five-year-old Václav, and founder of Barrandov Studios, "the Czech Hollywood," who also owned a movie theater that she used to visit as a little girl (with raspberry candy smeared on her face to make her look grownup). Now he was wriggling like an eel to rescue Czech cinema at his own studio, where the Nazis had taken 51 percent of the shares away from him. His diplomacy was successful: of forty Czech movies made in the period from 1939 to 1945, not a single one had Nazi content. (Though it wasn't possible to show Jews in a positive light, and students were a taboo topic. In 1939, after demonstrations on the national holiday, the Germans had closed down all the Czech colleges, and 1,200 students had immediately ended up in concentration camps. The Czechs were meant to be nothing but a German workforce.)

In the Protectorate, Baarová made her four best Czech movies, in all of which she played vamps.* She also received offers from Italy, and acted in movies directed by Enrico Guazzoni and Vittorio de Sica.

Another person in Lída's circle was the actress Adina Mandlová, the friend who didn't want her ashes to spoil anybody's garden.

One day, Lída and Adina were having a conversation about men. Lída joked that the concert hall at the Lucerna wouldn't be big enough for a gathering of all her lovers.

"You'd have to hire the whole stadium at Strahov," said Mandlová, "with the rallying cry, 'Every Czech should go to Strahov at least once in his life!' "

At the time, two Czechs were trying to get her attention, the head of President Hácha's chancellery and the minister of industry. One of them apparently said: "That's a woman with class. Power attracts her, and the loss of it repels her."

We don't know if she satisfied the minister's hopes. Baarová was discreet. What we do know about her emotional and sexual life was forced out of her.

In April 1945, once the Red Army had reached Bratislava, Lída was warned that she must escape. "But I haven't harmed

---

* Including three directed by Otakar Vávra: *Dívka v modrém*, *Maskovana milenka* and *Turbína*.

anyone. The Germans didn't want anything to do with me—they were the ones who threw me out of the movies. And it all happened before the war began!" she explained. She couldn't foresee that as soon as some of the Nazis disappeared after the war, she would be regarded as someone who knew their secrets.

However, when more than two million Germans began to flee from Bohemia, she left by car with a family she had befriended. They stopped at a village. The Americans had blown up the bridges and she couldn't get all the way to Munich. For a month she helped in the fields of the farmer with whom she was staying. There she met an American soldier called Peter, who fell in love.

She let Peter and his fellow soldiers watch as she bathed in a stream.

Peter and his fellow soldiers were part of the Counterintelligence Corps, forerunner of the CIA.

Then Peter's boss, intelligence officer Major Malsch, fell in love with her. She left the soldier and moved into the major's villa in Munich, where they lived together for more than two months, while he mixed her favorite cocktails and never stopped asking questions.

After her arrest, the Americans told Baarová that Goebbels and his wife had poisoned their six children and then committed suicide. Then they informed her that she was on a list of war criminals, and sent her back to Czechoslovakia.

Stanislav Motl spent ten years looking for the relevant documents all over Europe.

"There isn't a scrap of evidence to prove that Lída Baarová collaborated with the Reich during the war," he says. "Her crime was that she lived for her career and nothing else."

For her, the Nazis were a movie audience.

While Baarová was in a Prague jail, hearing the same two remarks again and again, "You stupid cow" and "You whore," her friend Adina Mandlová went off to visit some friends outside Prague.

Throughout the occupation, there had been a rumor going round that Mandlová was the lover of Karl Hermann Frank, the Reich minister for Bohemia and Moravia. In a small town called Beroun, a policeman spotted her and shouted: "The bird is flying after Frank!" Guards armed with bayonets dragged her across the marketplace, straight to the station, to transport her back to Prague. People for whom she had performed here a year earlier shouted: "Where's Frank when you need his help?" The crowd even threw stones at the train.

At the jail, news photographers were brought to see Adina, who was made to pose while doing physical labor.

After her acquittal in 1946, Adina Mandlová's health declined. She was often seen drunk. In Czech and German the word *Mandel* means "almond," so people started saying: "Baarová has *mandlové*/almond eyes, and Mandlová has *barové*/barroom eyes."

• • •

Two pieces of news reached the jail:

Lída's mother had died of a heart attack during her interrogation, as the interrogator continued to shout at her: "Where is Lída's jewelry?" She was fifty-six years old.

Her sister Zorka Janů was having a successful stage career. She was on her way to a rehearsal when her path was blocked by actor and communist Václav Vydra. "No sister of Lída Baarová can be a Czech actress!" he declared, and wouldn't let Zorka go inside the theater.

She drank gasoline, but her life was saved.

After his wife's funeral, Karel Babka ended up in the hospital. To stop the cancer from spreading higher up, his leg was amputated. When he returned home, he found that Zorka hadn't been eating; she was wasting away, and several times a day she suffered frenzied fits of obsessive bathing. She would dry herself and then get straight back into the bathtub again, constantly repeating: "I've got to be clean!"

He was making dinner when, from the corner of his eye, he saw a large towel fall from the bathroom window to the ground outside. He heard the towel land with a dull thud against the concrete steps. She was twenty-three years old.

Lída Baarová's problems after the war also resulted from the fact that her nation had a problem with itself.

In a country robbed of land by its neighbors, including Poland, the ordinary Czech performed his duty of "being a Czech"—just as Milena Jesenská had wished. He worked in order to survive. (The resistance movement promoted the slogan: "Work slowly.")

A Czech could either work for the Germans, or work for the Germans.

As soon as he graduated from high school in 1942, eighteen-year-old Josef Škvorecký—later a famous writer—was assigned a job at a munitions factory. He had the choice of an arms factory in Bremen, where there was constant carpet bombing, or a factory making parts for German Messerschmitts in his own peaceful town of Náchod.

He chose the job without air raids.

However, in a world of crime it's impossible to remain on the outside. Many things explain the attitude of the Czechs, but that doesn't mean they weren't affected by what happened. They bore a sense of shared guilt, though they may not have been aware of it.

They may have intuitively taken it out on Baarová and Mandlová—on people who, in their eyes, had communed with the executioner of their own free will.

Lída Baarová's life abhorred a vacuum.

Soon after her mother's and sister's deaths, two people came to the jail to see her. Both of them declared their love for her. She didn't know either of them at all well.

The first was Marcela Nepovímová, an actress five years younger than Lída. She brought some violets, and asked what she could do for her. "Take care of my daddy," Lída requested.

The second person was an actor ten years her junior called Jan Kopecký. He had reliable information that Baarová would soon be released without a trial. "And I shall be your husband," he announced.

Eighteen months later, Baarová left jail. The investigation had shown that she had only been in contact with the Nazis on career matters.

They were married in late July 1947, six months before the communists definitively took power.

After the wedding, Jan Kopecký was fired from his job, so they set up a two-person puppet theater and traveled about the country.

The communist putsch of 1948 was approaching when the phone rang at their home in Prague (still that same villa that looked like a ship). "You must run away, they're going to lock you up again!" somebody whispered and hung up. (To this day nobody knows who made the call.)

Jan wasn't at home, he was away with a friend. For several weeks the house had been under surveillance by secret agents. Marcela gave Lída an overcoat and she calmly went out. With no handbag, as if she were just going for a short walk. Once she had lost sight of the house, she started to run, and reached the apartment of a friend from jail.

Meanwhile, Kopecký called home to say that he'd been in a car crash, but Karel Babka pretended not to know him, saying that Baarová and Kopecký had gone to Moravia to look for work. Jan went to consult with Lída's friend from jail about what this could mean.

Baarová's fur coats had been confiscated and were still in police storage. Kopecký brought along a moth-eaten old fur, bribed the storehouse keeper, and managed to extract the "most stunning mink coat in the entire Protectorate." He sold it to raise the money to bribe three border guards.

During their escape, which was made to look like an

ordinary journey, Lída had her hair dyed blond and wore glasses with thick lenses.

They reached Salzburg with nothing but the clothes they were wearing. They got jobs at the Café Mozart. Lída became a barmaid. News of where the great star was serving cocktails quickly spread.

She is said to have made a fortune in tips.

She broke up with Kopecký.

She acted in five Spanish movies.

She acted in the young Fellini's *I Vitelloni*.

She was thirty-seven. Actresses younger than her were appearing in Italy—Sophia Loren and Gina Lollobrigida.

She married an Austrian doctor who owned a sanatorium.

Three years later, she was widowed.

In 1958, she left the movies, because of her outdated acting style.

She acted on stage in Hanover, Bonn, Vienna and Stuttgart. She was the most famous Czech actress in Europe, though in Czechoslovakia hardly anybody was aware of the fact.

Her final role (in 1982) was as the greatest anti-fascist of all actresses, Marlene Dietrich.

Press cuttings on Baarová at the Prague city library come to an end in 1948, and then start up again in 1990.

"She seems to have been on the censor's black list in Czechoslovakia for the longest time," I say.

"What do you mean?" responds movie critic Eva Za-
oralová, now artistic director of the Karlovy Vary Film
Festival.

"What? Wasn't she on it?"

"No, because there was no list of names that couldn't be
written or mentioned aloud."

"So how did people know there was a ban?"

"Everyone had to sense intuitively whose name couldn't
be mentioned."

For example, throughout the communist years, intuition
was responsible for the fact that the names of Jane Fonda and
Ingmar Bergman were never mentioned in public, because
they had demonstrated against the occupation of Czechoslovakia by Warsaw Pact troops in 1968.

Marcela Nepovímová, the admirer with the bunch of violets,
gave up acting to care for Karel Babka, who was twenty-three
years her senior. They got married. The amputation of his leg
didn't protect him from cancer, and he died twelve years later.
Afterwards, she said their love had been worth more than all
the roles she might still have been offered.

The state had appropriated their house shaped like a ship.
Marcela and Karel were ordered to move to a small village in
Sudetenland. It was winter, and they went to live in a tumble-
down shack with no heating. As a bourgeois civil servant,
Karel didn't qualify for a coal ration. Marcela used to go into
the woods with a saw. She worked at a factory making artificial jewelry. Under a false name, Lída sent them parcels.

Once Marcela had buried her husband, she went back to

Prague. After years of trying to get a passport, in 1982 the authorities allowed her to go abroad. She found Lída in Salzburg and took care of her. Baarová didn't know how to cook or clean. After breakfast and a walk, she would come home and rest on the sofa. In summer, she would walk on her own private beach on the shore of a lake.

When she came to Prague after 1989, Lída stayed at Marcela's apartment. Marcela lived in a block. For three days Lída hesitated over whether to go outside, but the small space—four hundred square feet—was unbearable. She went out.

She went to Wenceslas Square, knowing (as she later said in an interview) that whatever ill people spoke of her, it was bound to be too little.

Crowds of fans came to her public appearance at the concert hall in the Lucerna Palace. The first questions in every interview were always about Goebbels.

Two years later, as she sat on the sofa in Salzburg, waiting for death, she told Helena Třeštíková that her daddy often used to say: " 'Lída, whatever may happen, just keep going.'

"And that's how it always was, I just kept going. But now I don't want to keep going anymore. I refuse."

After her death, it turned out that Lída had left her entire estate to a gardener from a nearby monastery.

He was fifty-two, and she was eighty-three when, as her fan, he came for an autograph. He declared his love for her. Marcela said he was too young. Lída was offended. "But he's fallen in love," she told her second mother. "And when you're in Prague he makes me soup."

Two years before her death, she stopped recognizing either of them.

On February 9, 2001, in the Main Hall at Strašnice Crematorium in Prague, her fans said farewell to her with this justification: "Oh well, she was just a woman."

More than likely, nobody mentioned that those who had brought about her downfall were only men.

HOW ARE YOU COPING WITH THE GERMANS?

It's 1939.

"So how are you doing?" the journalist Milena Jesenská asks a farmer near the town of Slaný.

"I've gotten the potatoes planted, and the rye's sown. We had a cold spring, but miraculously everything has come up, beautifully. I think I'll cut down two of the old apple trees in the orchard and plant new ones. The duck already has young—go take a look at them, they're like dandelion clocks. I must give that lilac bush a pruning so it won't wither, to make the garden beautiful this year," replies the farmer.

"But how are you coping with the Germans?" asks Jesenská, refusing to give in.

"Oh, whatever, they come by, and I get on with my work," the farmer replies calmly.

"Aren't you at all afraid?"

"Why should I be afraid?" he wonders sincerely, and suddenly retorts: "Besides, lady, a man can only die once. And if he dies a little sooner, he's just dead for a little longer."

PROOF OF LOVE

PART 1: ETERNITY LASTS FOR EIGHT YEARS

Mrs. Kvítková the goose plucker plucked seventy-two geese in eight hours and went into the history books.

At an academic conference in Brno, Minister of Information Václav Kopecký said that Europe's highest mountain was Mount Elbrus, and defined the previously held view that it was Mont Blanc as "a relic of reactionary cosmopolitanism."

A definitive list was compiled of authors who would never be published again, including Dickens, Dostoevsky, Nietzsche and several hundred others.

The poet Michal Sedloň wrote that "nourishment" and "production" were now poetic words.

The number of individual copies of books destroyed in the country during these years is estimated at twenty-seven million.

As Prime Minister Antonín Zápotocký diagnosed the new age: "It's impossible to live the old way—now life is better and happier!"

In two years—at Stalin's suggestion—the most eminent leaders will be condemned to the gallows.

At the Zlatá Husa hotel on Wenceslas Square—where Andersen wrote his most famous fairytale about the idle rich, *The Princess and the Pea*—there hung a sign that said: "With the Soviet Union Forever."

79

Every day at midnight, at the end of its broadcast, Radio Prague played the Soviet national anthem.

This is how the 1940s end and the '50s begin in Czechoslovakia.

As part of the celebrations for Joseph Stalin's seventieth birthday held in December 1949,* the authorities decide that nine million of the country's population of fourteen million citizens will sign birthday wishes for him.

They manage to collect the signatures in four days. To mark the occasion, a decision is taken to erect the world's largest statue of Stalin on a hill above the Vltava River in Prague.

No sculptor can refuse to take part in the competition. Fifty-four artists are given nine months to design a statue. Thank God, the top Czechoslovak sculptor Ladislav Šaloun is lucky enough to be dead (as they say about this particular death in Prague). In order not to win, Karel Pokorný, regarded as Šaloun's successor, draws the leader with his arms spread in a friendly gesture, making Stalin look like Christ.

Most of the other artists make the same mistake. "They

---

* Joseph Vissarionovich Stalin should have celebrated his seventieth birthday in 1948. It seems that he falsely gave 1879 as his date of birth in many documents, and thus it was accepted as the official date during his lifetime. This is discussed by Russian historian Edvard Radzinsky in his book, *Stalin: The First In-depth Biography Based on Explosive New Documents from Russia's Secret Archives* (Doubleday, 1996).

have presented Stalin in an affected way," says the panel of judges.

Fifty-six-year-old Otakar Švec, son of a confectioner who specializes in sculptures made of sugar, is a frustrated sculptor.

After a strong debut, when as a student he sculpted a motorcyclist and successfully captured movement in stone, he designed a statue of the father of the republic, T. G. Masaryk, and then a statue of Jan Hus. Both were destroyed by the fascists during the war. After the war, he designed a statue of Roosevelt, but never completed it, because the communists took power. Before the war, he used to exhibit his avant-garde sculptures in the West. He thought he would never get another commission.

Now—so rumor has it—Otakar Švec throws together a model under the influence of a couple of bottles of vodka. He is a decent man, so he deliberately plagiarizes a well-known pre-war idea for a statue of Miroslav Tyrš, a bourgeois public benefactor whom the communists don't like.

Unfortunately, he wins.

Stalin is standing at the head of a group of people. In one hand, he holds a book, and he rests the other hand on his chest, under his coat.

On the left—Soviet—side, Stalin is followed by a worker holding a flag, then an agrobiologist, then a female partisan and finally a Soviet soldier who is looking round behind him.

On the right—Czechoslovak—side of Stalin comes: a worker with a flag, a woman from the countryside, a scientist and a Czechoslovak soldier also looking backwards.

Some people start to whisper boldly that "there's Stalin with everyone crawling up his ass."

Just one of his buttons—they say—will be the size of a loaf of bread.

The monument will be one hundred feet high, and Stalin fifty feet wide, altogether the size of a ten-story pre-war building. His foot alone will be over six feet long.

The whole thing, made of granite (not at all suitable for sandstone Prague, but unlike sandstone, granite lasts for centuries) is to stand on Letná hill and provide competition for the castle. Its vast scale is to crush the past. It will be visible from the Old Town Square, and will stand on the other side of Čechův Bridge, across the river from the top of Pařížská Street.

To make a Stalin of this kind, 260 blocks of granite are needed, each well over six feet by six feet by six feet in size.

The fact that a quarry is found with thick enough walls from which to cut out such large blocks of stone of exactly the same color is little short of a miracle.

The two architects helping Švec—a married couple called Štursa—have to devise a way to prepare the weak sandstone hill for this colossus.

They decide that the hill will be filled from the inside with gigantic blocks of concrete, which will form something like underground halls.

Two years after the competition is announced, people start to voice their concerns about the statue. Švec's sketches, models and drawings are exhibited to the citizens for their consultation, and a debate is held about "Prague's new jewel."

"I'm worried that from a distance the figures will merge into one and Stalin won't be sufficiently visible."

"Why are the last figures in line looking backwards? I find that too avant-garde," people say, as the doubts increase.

"They're looking back for ideological reasons," replies Švec. "It's to do with the guarantee of living in peace, it's about defense. They're also looking round for compositional reasons, so the monument will have a nice view from the back, not the rear end of a soldier."

"Why as an artist do you want to defend our people on the monument, comrade?"

"A rearguard defense is necessary so that the people in the vanguard can feel calm," explains the sculptor.

Later on, people will say that the figures behind Stalin are standing in line for meat.

Many citizens are still implacable. "As a symbol, we find the monument disturbing. It's not a joyful, faithful depiction, but instead looks like a tombstone," four people who signed the exhibition visitors' book noted.

"Whom is Comrade Stalin leading? The people are literally creeping after him as if they're up against a wall. The design should be torn up and a new competition announced."

"The monument will be in bad taste. More care should be devoted to the depiction of one of the greatest giants in history."

Otakar Švec doesn't yet know that he is a prisoner.

• • •

The models posing for the monument were apparently extras from the Barrandov Film Studios.

Later, it was said that the man who posed as Stalin drank himself to death. Nobody knew his name, but the whole of Prague called him "Stalin," and his psyche couldn't take it.

Švec and the architects build a series of models of the monument in clay. First, three feet high, then ten.

The Party and the government have their eye on Švec. The record of comments made about him at a meeting between the authorities and the artist on January 4, 1951, fills twelve typewritten pages.

The figure of Stalin isn't towering over the rest of the monument! Prime Minister Zápotocký says that it should already be plain to see in the clay models that this is a monument to Stalin—a courageous man. "Now that he's getting down to work, perhaps the artist is starting to be afraid of his own ideas," he adds.

Zápotocký and eight of his ministers discuss whether to lower the figures behind Stalin, or raise the leader on an extra pedestal.

The monument must not look like a sarcophagus from afar!

The figures behind Stalin are too decorative.

Can't the artist take a more profound approach to his work?

Why does he refuse to make more clay models and show them to the authorities?

Finally, the prime minister concludes that Otakar Švec is indeed afraid of his own monument.

The sculptor doesn't hear all of this; he and his colleagues are invited to join the meeting forty-five minutes later. First the architect, Vlasta Štursová, gives her explanation: they have deliberately not raised the figure of Stalin, because that would mean distancing him from the people, but in fact he is leading the people, and they stem from him.

Švec explains to the authorities that if they wish for Stalin to be different in height from the rest, the monument will have two different scales. "From the artistic point of view, that is untenable," he says.

The government buys him a bigger studio, because his old one is turning out to be too small. Now, Party representatives will hold their meetings at his workshop.

They come with their own penknives.

Each time, they stick them in the clay and trim down the heads of the people behind Stalin.

The first man with a penknife is the minister with radical views on Mont Blanc and Mount Elbrus.

Wielding the second penknife is the most virulent of them all, Professor Zdeněk Nejedlý, author of *The History of Czech Music*. He was an art historian, and had even been a democrat; during the occupation he illegally escaped to Moscow and became a professor there. He came back to become a theoretician of everything in socialist Czechoslovakia.

In 1951, he is minister of schools, the sciences, and the arts. He writes a famous essay about new art and love. "People will still fall in love," he predicts, "but we expect that, under socialism, as the working class, they will love each other more and better than before. They'll no longer come up with any of that fake stuff about 'unhappy love affairs,' or the sensual deterioration in which bourgeois romance so often wallowed."

For instance, he can't bear the fact that Czechoslovakia was famous before the war for avant-garde photography. When he sees shadows or smoke photographed out of context in Jaroslav Rössler's photographs from the 1920s, he flies into a rage.

(When Stalin dies, Nejedlý will state that from now on the Czech monument makes the most important statement about the Father of Nations: Stalin lives forever.)

Four months after the first reprimand, Švec receives another. The authorities upbraid him again in 1952, in 1953 and in 1954.

Four years go by, the stonemasons have been working on the blocks of granite for a long time now, the scaffolding and the crane are in place, and the artist is still being advised to "soften and change some of the figures, so they won't look despotic." Švec takes women back to his studio and drinks with them.

He comes forward with explanations.

A year before the monument is unveiled, his wife can't bear the situation any longer, and turns on the gas in the bathroom.

Švec finds her dead in the bathtub.

• • •

New doubts arise, which luckily have nothing to do with the sculptor. The concern is that it looks as if the stone Stalin has come to Prague, stopped at the river and is gazing at the wonderful city.

However, he has come from the east, so why is he standing on the western riverbank?

If he were on his way in, he would have to stop at the river, but with his back to the city. So he's not on his way in.

If he isn't entering the city, perhaps he's leaving it?

But for what reason?

What doesn't he like about socialist Prague?

Has he only just crossed the Vltava and is already turning back?

Why is he looking east?

Or perhaps he has in fact entered the city, and is merely looking behind him out of nostalgia?

From the hundreds of pages typed on Czechoslovak typewriters, pages filled with comments about the monument and then treated as classified, it appears that the proliferation of doubts is a race without a finish line—nobody can possibly predict when and how it will end. And each idea can instantly change into its own contradiction.

It is the spring of 1955, more than two years since Stalin's death.

The monument is to be unveiled on May 1. A seventeen-page deed of erection has been prepared, which not only states that from now on the Father of Nations presides over Prague, but also stresses that Stalin "is looking at the Bethlehem Chapel."

A remarkable statement for the communist era.

This is the chapel where Jan Hus preached his sermons. Communist propaganda has appropriated religion: it says Hus was a revolutionary, the Hussites were the first communist organization, and their pillaging expeditions were nothing more than disinterested incitement of the local peoples to fight against feudalism.

Now, between Stalin on Letná hill and Hus in the chapel on Bethlehem Square, an almost visible red thread is to be stretched.

The sculptor knows that his monument is aesthetically hideous. Pompous and overblown.

He knows the authorities don't like the monument either, but for different reasons. They are so disgusted with the sculptor that by now they only communicate with him through the architects.

But the press gushes: "From the ideological point of view, this is the only composition that shows Generalissimus Stalin as a statesman, a builder, a victorious leader, a teacher of the people, and at the same time as Comrade Stalin and Stalin the man, as one of us."

It is evening, some time before the unveiling.

Otakar Švec leaves his studio, takes a cab, and goes to Letná hill to look at the monument incognito.

He asks the cab driver what he thinks about it.

"I'll show you something," says the cab driver. "Take a good look at the Soviet side."

"What's there?"

"I think you can see it. The partisan girl has her hand on the soldier's fly."

"What?"

"I'm telling you, sir, when they unveil it, the guy who designed it is one-hundred-percent sure to get shot."

Otakar Švec goes back to his studio and commits suicide.

News of his death is kept secret; nobody is allowed to publicize it.

The name Švec does not appear on the monument.

On May 1, 1955, during the unveiling ceremony, it is announced that the monument was created by the Czechoslovak People.

There are rumors about victims.

"A total of seven people were killed during construction," the sacristan went on. "The first was the sculptor who designed this statue, and the last was the unskilled laborer who arrived on Monday, still well-oiled, and a board on the sixth floor broke under him—he fell head downwards and was killed when he hit the statue's little finger."

In fact, the sacristan from Bohumil Hrabal's story "The Treachery of Mirrors" is wrong. Prague's Stalin had no protruding finger. If somebody was killed, maybe he hit the whole hand.

•   •   •

The statue stands there for almost eight years, until 1962.

It outlives the thaw of 1956 and the condemnation of Stalin by seven years!

He is condemned, but only in the USSR, Poland and Hungary. French historian Muriel Blaive wrote a book about 1956 in Czechoslovakia entitled *Une déstalinisation manquée* ("A Missed Opportunity for Destalinization").

There is an astonishing lack of strong reactions to what is happening in the neighboring countries, and the regime in Prague even digs itself in more firmly. For example, as we know from Security Service reports, in private conversations people are saying things like "we should implore God not to let those beasts from Hungary come here, because they'd kill us all." Attempts at student demonstrations don't prompt any major public response.

Whereas there is a demonstration of loyalty to the Soviet Union, and the Soviet ambassador is greeted by 25,000 people in Prague. "The Czech government itself is surprised by society's conformism," reports a correspondent for *Journal de Genève*.

Why?

Three years earlier, monetary reform was introduced, which for the average citizen proved to be a swindle, so people came out onto the streets and a large number of industrial plants went on strike. There was no Stalin around anymore to threaten a third world war, so to improve the nation's sense of well-being, Czechoslovakia's arms factories switched to manufacturing television sets, gramophones and refrigerators. Now the market is flooded with goods.

GOTTLAND   91

On the day when Khrushchev delivers his famous secret speech at the Twentieth Congress of the Soviet Communist Party, President Zápotocký (the man who as prime minister had supervised Švec's work), who has been invited to attend, has a meeting in Moscow with Czech and Slovak students. The students have been here for some time, and they already know that Khrushchev regards Stalin as a murderer, so they want to talk to their leader about this.

"Do you really want to poke around in all that?" asks the president. "The right policy is not to interfere," he adds.

The team of Stalin's faithful disciples from Prague has a problem. In Moscow, people talk openly about his crimes, but the Czech visitors have no interest in publicizing Khrushchev's speech on their return home—that would mean their own end.

Besides, there is nobody in Czechoslovakia capable of assuming the new leadership, nobody like Poland's Władysław Gomułka, first secretary of the Party and de facto leader of the country.

A newsreel.

The journalist asks a middle-aged man walking past Letná hill what heroism means today. "Once upon a time, brave men went to war," she says, and thrusts the microphone his way.

Laborer Josef Král thinks for a while, and then says: "These days, heroism means doing everything that's demanded of us."

This we know: in order to survive in unfavorable circumstances, a small nation has to adapt. It has carried this down from the days of the Habsburgs and the Protectorate of Bohemia and Moravia.

Writer Pavel Kohout points out that, after the war in Czechoslovakia, there were no Soviet troops, there was no putsch, the communists had genuine support, and in the 1946 elections they gained more than 40 percent of the votes. In 1938, the Czech nation had experienced annexation and occupation, and had been betrayed by Great Britain and France, so when the communists took power, it looked as if the Soviet Union was their only reliable means of support.

Besides, a hundred years earlier František Palacký, the man who awakened Czech national consciousness, predicted that if the Czechs ever moved closer to Russia, it would be an act of desperation on their part.

"That's why, later on," says Pavel Kohout, "it was so hard to admit to those who had supported the communists that they had unwittingly done the devil a favor. And of course it all happened very quickly."

Underneath Stalin, in the concrete spaces inside the hill, prostitutes receive their clients. Earlier, a famous painter kept a folding bed in there. But only until it came out that he was taking underage girls there. Earlier still, tons of potatoes were stored there.

In 1961, Moscow holds another Party Congress and Khrushchev is still criticizing Stalinism.

Stalin's mummified body is removed from Lenin's mausoleum on Red Square, and Zápotocký's successor as president of Czechoslovakia, Antonín Novotný, must respond to this.

In 1952, he had personally divided among himself and his colleagues the valuables left behind by their comrades who died on the gallows. Now he must be ready to rehabilitate them and admit that the Party was wrong.

The monument that stands "forever" was another mistake.

The man who is to eliminate Stalin—engineer Vladimír Křížek—hears the strangest sentence of his entire life from the authorities: "You are to demolish the monument, but with dignity."

The top expert at an elite engineering enterprise, Křížek asks them to explain. The monument is a concrete monster, clad in granite, and it is fixed to the inside of the mountain by a reinforced concrete structure. Nobody foresaw that it would ever have to be destroyed. It can only be blown up.

"Destroy it in a dignified way, so that the gravity of the USSR isn't harmed," the secretary of the district Party committee instructs him, and spells out the conditions.

No explosive materials may be placed inside Stalin's head.

Nobody is to fire at it.

No gunshots are to be heard at all.

Nobody is to talk about it, film it or photograph it. Anyone who breaks this rule will be arrested on the spot.

Engineer Křížek's entire enterprise is paralyzed with fear.

The grounds are strictly guarded day and night. The whole thing will be blown up, but someone has the idea of taking the head apart manually. Two stonemasons (father and son) are suspended from it, chipping off five-inch chunks at a time with hammers. They dare not throw them to the ground, so they are removed by hoist.

The explosion is prepared by the country's best pyrotechnician, Jiří Příhoda. He knows that any mistake could send half the downtown area sky-high.

He spends two weeks thinking, and not sleeping; now and then he just drifts off for three minutes. He prepares 2,100 charges.

He wants to blast the whole monument in one go, but he is pressured by the military, whom the government has sent along just in case. They force him to do it in three stages—they are afraid pieces of the monument will fly out over the city and kill people. They dog him every step of the way, never letting him concentrate and constantly nagging him.

First, Jiří Příhoda has a fit of hysterics and starts shouting. Then he downs six glasses of slivovitz and presses the firing button.

When it's all over he sits on the grass, weeping loudly.

An ambulance takes him away to the mental hospital.

The explosions were a great success. Clearing the metal and concrete from the surrounding area takes a year.

Not a single line about the monument's destruction appears in the press.

Prague's monument to Stalin never existed.

PART 2: LIFE-SAVING FRUIT JUICE

Stalin left behind a thirty-six-foot-high pedestal. Nowadays, there is a metronome on it. The big red pointer oscillates from the Soviet side to the Czechoslovak side and back again. Skateboarders rampage around it, and on the old steps, some-one has used white paint to try to communicate with some-one else, writing: it-wont-work-katerinarybova@seznam.cz.

Sometimes there are no sponsors to pay for the electricity, so the pointer comes to a standstill.

"Look, time has stopped again," people say.

But that's not a good metaphor for this place—quite the opposite.

Because time has picked up so much speed that Otakar Švec's death, for instance, ten years after the Second World War ended, feels as if it happened in the days of cuneiform script.

I've always been bothered by the fact that the Czechs have never written a reliable history of the rise and fall of the great-est proof of love in communist Europe.

However, it turns out that to do this you have to become an archeologist.

When, at the Central Archive of the Czech Republic, I am handed a file marked *Stalinův památník v Praze* ("The Stalin monument in Prague") with stamps on the documents which show that they were only declassified three days ago, I feel a pleasant thrill—it was done at my request, nobody has taken an interest in them before.

There are dozens of protocols about the monument, many of them marked "Confidential." But there's nothing about the victims of the construction work or anything else about the sculptor, apart from the fact that he was horribly oppressed. Not a word about him having ended his own life.

If he really was found in his studio, the secret police must have gone in there. They must have questioned his neighbors, they must have sniffed about, so there ought to be at least a note about it. They must have written down the circumstances in which the body was found.

I put in a request to search the archives of the former Security Service for Otakar Švec's file. From October 2003 until January 2004, I wait for a response.

They reply that they can't find a single sheet of paper with his name on it.

Sculptor Olbram Zoubek says Otakar Švec gassed himself, just as his wife did, in the bathroom. (This may be true, as for many years Zoubek had an employee called Junek, who worked in stucco and was Švec's loyal assistant.)

Television documentary director Martin Skyba says he shot himself. (He may be well informed, as he makes historical documentaries.)

An art historian called Petr Wittlich who specializes in that era says the sculptor hanged himself. (This may also be true, as Professor Wittlich wrote the one and only monograph on Švec not long after his death.)

"But where did he do it?"

"In his studio, in the loft of the Koruna Palace on Wenceslas Square."

I spend three days trying to find out if the sculptor really did have a studio at the Koruna. He did not. He had two, but not downtown—besides, there's no trace of Švec left in either. I tell this to the professor.

"I wrote about him, but I didn't know him personally. He had no children, and you won't find anybody in Prague who knew him because they must've all died by now."

Despite some Frankovka red wine, Jiří Příhoda, the explosives expert, is economical with his words. If I hadn't known in advance that he was taken off to the hospital, I'm sure he would never have mentioned it.

"That was the most dreadful event in my entire life, demolishing that thing, though I had some tough assignments afterwards too. But there's no point in going back to it," he says. "So much pain . . ."

We don't go back to it.

Yet, a week later, in a little-known novel called *Café Slavia*, I come across a description of the explosion. It was written by Ota Filip, a writer who in 1960 was forced by the regime to become a miner.

I call the explosives expert. I tell him I have found something about his explosion.

Next morning, Mr. Příhoda's wife informs me in the hallway that last night was hell. "Who could have written that?" he kept repeating, trembling all over.

"But it's 2003," I say.

"What difference does it make?" asks his wife.

I read out loud: " 'The next night there was a full moon. The Vltava looked like a silver snake that had lain down to sleep beneath the bridges. And then there was an earthquake.' "

"Well, well . . ." says Mr. Příhoda, clutching at his heart.

" 'A gray cloud of smoke shielded Stalin right up to the neck. Suddenly it lit up with all the colors of the rainbow. His head was still protruding amid that strange light, but he tipped forwards, as some dreadful force broke his neck. Stones drummed on the roofs and fell into the Vltava, opaque by now. The echo of the explosion returned to the city and broke through the cloud of dust which was hanging over the downtown area like a gray bell.' "

"But the explosions were in the daytime!" Příhoda rages.

" 'Then silence fell. Only Helena von Molwitzová screamed and fell to the ground. She wasn't found until morning, lying on the lawn . . .' "

"Good God, what are you reading?"

" 'They carried her into the embassy on a stretcher. Her face was covered in blood.' "

Jiří Příhoda can't get over it. "Only one man was killed during the demolition, and that was before the explosion. He was from the committee. He went into the chambers underneath the monument, stood on a plank in the wrong place, fell over and never got up again. Why on earth invent other victims?"

"Because Stalin demands victims," explains his wife.

"They once wrote that his head fell off and rolled down the bridge into the marketplace. And then I get blamed for it all!"

"Straight after Stalin he had a heart attack," Mrs. Příhodová tells me. "Ever since he'd had sleepless nights for two weeks before the explosion, my husband hasn't slept properly, for forty-one years."

"I fall asleep, like last night, for five minutes. And then I have a dream, I don't know what it's about, I just know I grit my teeth and say: 'I won't allow it!' "

In its weekend edition, the newspaper *Lidové noviny* publishes my small ad, with a photograph of the models who posed for Švec. I came across their picture in Prague's Museum of Communism, but I couldn't find their names.

I write that I am looking for these people, or relatives of theirs.

Five letters arrive. All more or less about the fact that somebody has very troublesome neighbors and asking if I could do something about it.

Two years ago, Czech television showed some footage taken by a daredevil who illegally filmed the explosion on an amateur camera. There was a reminder that the totalitarian state was just as afraid of cameras as it was of firearms.

He is a Mr. M., the same age as everyone concerned, around eighty. He is wearing a tartan jacket and a cravat. He shows me a magazine for which he writes about Moravian wines.

"A friend and I filmed the explosion. He had an eight-millimeter camera, and we hid in the bushes on the hill opposite. One filmed, the other kept watch. The friend was my foreman, because we'd worked together as laborers building a tunnel, right next to Stalin."

"What sort of laborers?" I ask, glancing at the cravat and the magazine about wine.

"I was a road worker."

"With a camera?"

"I mean I was a workman in the mornings, and at night I wrote the screenplays for TV programs, under a pseudonym of course. I was already middle-aged when I graduated in journalism. But I really don't want to talk about it."

"But you've already started."

"All right, I'll finish: I had to be a workman, and please don't badger me about it."

"Why not?"

"Those are things best not mentioned," he says, and lowers his voice, as if somebody undesirable might really be listening. We are talking at the Café Arco, where Kafka used to sit, and where the Ministry of Internal Affairs later had its own canteen.

Mr. M. fetches out a file with a photograph of the Soviet side of the monument.

"You see, I set up the camera to get the best possible shot of the partisan girl's gesture as she grabs the soldier." He shows me. "Some people were informed that Švec killed himself because of that fly."

"Who told them that?"

"I think about fifteen of Prague's cab drivers said, naturally in the greatest confidence, that they had driven him up to the monument that night."

The sculptor Olbram Zoubek is seventy-seven years old, an energetic man who has no ungrounded fears.

He was a student when Švec was working on Stalin.

After the self-immolation of history student Jan Palach in 1969, Zoubek managed to get inside the morgue and make two death masks of the national hero, who was being guarded by a whole herd of secret policemen, and so too shall I succeed in discovering some facts about Švec.

Zoubek knows a sculptor who worked with Otakar Švec on Stalin, and whose name is Josef Vajce. He is the only man still alive who knew him personally.

Fantastic!

To make sure I don't give the old man a shock, Zoubek calls him at home for me.

"Listen, Honza," he says, "there's a guy from Poland here who's going to call you in an hour . . ." ("He'll see you," he mutters across to me.)

I leave Zoubek's place, and in an hour the phone is answered by a man who sounds elderly.

"I'm afraid Mr. Vajce has been away in Ukraine for a week and I'm not at all sure when he'll be back."

I have found a list of the names of the radio commentators and technicians who worked on a live broadcast from the unveiling ceremony.

Most of them aren't in the phone book, but several are still alive.

"We know you well, brave partisan, raising your head on our monument . . ." said editor Sylvie Moravcová.

"I can hardly hear you," she says today, "because I've gone deaf, there's no point in you coming to see me, I can't remember anything, unless you'd like a glass of fruit juice!"

"Lines of people are slowly ascending the steps, paying tribute to the great Stalin and swearing to defend the freedom brought to us by the Soviet soldiers, and to make our homeland a paradise on earth," said editor Vladimír Brunát. "I'm eighty-five now and I'm blind, on top of which I'm in a wheelchair, but I'm happy to help," he says today. "The designer? I reported on the unveiling, but I'm sure I never knew the sculptor's name. There was no talk of any suicide. What's that you're saying? Nothing was known about it at the time."

Taking note of linguistic details in the Czech Republic can offer clues. Thus, in a situation where someone ought to say: "I was afraid to talk about it," "I hadn't the courage to ask about it," or "I had no idea about it," they say:

"THERE WAS NO TALK about it."

"NOTHING WAS KNOWN about it."

"That WASN'T ASKED about."

I often hear the impersonal form when people have to talk about communism. As if people had no influence on anything and were unwilling to take personal responsibility. As if to remind me that they were just part of a greater whole, which also had some sin of denial on its conscience.

I mention the Czechs' reluctance to remember the past to my friend Piotr Lipiński, who has been writing about the executioners and victims of Stalinism for years.

"It's out of fear," he says.

"Fifty years on? Nowadays, when they shouldn't be afraid of anything?"

"All the people you met are about eighty. The last fifteen years of independence are just an episode in their lives. Too short a time for them to be sure that it's a permanent state of affairs and can't change."

Prague's monument to Stalin does exist.

VICTIM OF LOVE

In the summer of 2006, I get an e-mail from an employee of the archive at the Czech Ministry of Internal Affairs. He writes that he has finally managed to find a file inscribed "Suicide of the artist Švec."

When the Security Service investigators and agents broke down the door (double locked, with the keys on the inside) of Švec's apartment, the sculptor was lying on the same sofa bed as his wife had been when she poisoned herself (and so he had not found her dead in the bathtub, as rumor had it).

The blinds were down. They could smell gas in the air.

On the table, he had left a letter to a notary called Dr. Dvořák.

The letter began with the sentence: "I am going after my wife Vlasta, and I am leaving my entire property, including the final installment for the Stalin monument, to the rank-and-file soldiers who lost their sight in the war." He asked for his body to be cremated using money left in the house, and for his car to be sold.

He didn't write a word about what had compelled him to commit suicide.

The investigators tracked down the notary. He turned out to be a friend of Švec's. "Vlasta did a good thing by poisoning herself," the sculptor had said to the notary. "At least she won't grow old. Why should I bother unveiling the monument if she's not here?"

He had apparently complained to the notary that he had dreamed of being appointed a professor, but hadn't been. He had also expected to be given a State Prize, but hadn't been awarded one.

A sculptor who worked with Švec on the monument told the investigators that "without a doubt, the specialists' comments on his work had an influence on his death." Additionally, Švec had heard people saying that he was too costly an artist, and that for the money assigned to his monument they could have built two housing estates for workers.

The sculptor also said that Švec was worried that the hill underneath Stalin was too weak, that it should be reinforced with concrete fill, and that it might collapse under the colossus he had designed.

The cleaning woman who looked after his apartment had noticed "the master" was nervous. Apparently, he had told her that lately Minister Kopecký "had come to hate him for some reason and no longer paid him as much attention as before, and that Vlasta had shown him the way."

Second Lieutenant Kraus, who conducted the inquiry, conveyed the following official explanation to his superiors: "Otakar Švec's suicide was brought about by the death of his wife, loneliness, and critical comments about his work which were made by some experts."

Among his documents, prescriptions for anti-depressants were found, and "photographs of several highly placed people from the USA."

The militia broke into the sculptor's apartment on April 21, 1955 (nine days before the monument was unveiled). He had committed suicide on March 3—that was the date on the letter, and that was the conclusion the inquiry came to. (Later on—for reasons unclear to me—dictionaries and encyclopedias gave the date of his death as April 4.)

Otakar Švec was lying dead in his apartment for fifty days. All that time, the gas was escaping.

And so for fifty days, in the run-up to the unveiling of the largest Stalin on the entire planet, nobody was actually interested in the whereabouts of its creator.

MRS. NOT-A-FAKE

It's 2004.

We're noisy, casually dressed. We've come from the West and we're striding the streets with patent insatiability.

We've already got mugs with Kafka on them.

We've got Kafka T-shirts.

We've got matchboxes.

We've got cartoon versions of his life story tucked under our arms and a 177-page summary of all his works. We're hanging out in the Jewish district, which is mainly a fake version of itself.

Over a hundred years ago, all the houses here were demolished, and the holes in the ground were covered in disinfectant. Once the Jews had been removed, bourgeois Germans and Czechs put up their grand tenements. Now we've stopped outside the house where he was born, though it's not the same house, but a different one, a fake version of it.

We're studying the menu displayed at the entrance, listing the dishes on offer at the Franz Kafka restaurant. Although this place was only established in 2003, and just looks like a restaurant from a hundred years ago.

Then we move a few hundred yards further on, down Široka Street. To the Café Franz Kafka, which, though it was opened in 2000, is also doing a perfect job of posing as a hundred-year-old café. On the wall hangs a photograph of the kind he could have absentmindedly left here: it's of him and his beloved sister, Ottla. The one who, in his opinion, was better off than he was both in health and self-confidence.

Now we've got sachets of sugar with Kafka on them (!) and at last we can feel satisfied. Even if it all turns out to be fake.

The most sophisticated among us come here in spring or fall. Maybe they've read somewhere that "Prague requires mist," and that in those seasons there's a chance of seeing the streets glistening with moisture, the lamplight muffled by fog, and the mood of mystery we demand when we think of Kafka in Prague. Summer, sunshine and hot weather deprive the city of its metaphysical element.

We have no idea that five floors above us his niece is still alive.

Věra S., Ottla's daughter.

She is eighty-four and she is not a fake.

For eight years, she could see "the world's largest statue of Stalin" from her window; her house was the first in line, standing directly opposite it. Now she can see the Hotel Intercontinental. And if she were to go downstairs today, she would find out that on the ground floor of her building, there are ladies' denim jackets hanging on display, at a sale price of two hundred Euros.

Right now, she is sitting at home in a red sweatsuit.

She has white hair and a slightly olive-skinned, slender face, which now that old age has altered its features, looks like a man's face. The man in her looks exactly as he does in the pictures we know from the covers of his books.

She has never given an interview. She consistently refuses; not even American television was able to buy her confessions.

And she could tell some interesting stories.

Not necessarily about Kafka, whom she may not remember, as he died when she was three years old, but about her mother, Ottla, for instance. Her mother divorced her husband when persecution of the Jews began in the Protectorate. She did it first and foremost for her daughters, who would then be associated with their Catholic father, and not with their Jewish mother. In this way she saved their lives. She herself was transported in 1942 to the camp at Terezín, and from there, as an escort for 1,196 Jewish children from Białystok, she arrived in Auschwitz, where they were all sent straight to the gas chamber.

Věra S.'s husband was an eminent translator of Shakespeare who drowned in the sea while on vacation in Bulgaria. She herself was an editor at a publishing firm and a translator from German.

Sometimes Věra S. used to lend out her surname.

It was borrowed from her by her fellow translators who had fallen from grace and were not entitled to publish. In Czechoslovakia, this way of doing your colleagues a good turn was called "covering." A *pokrývač* is a roofer, who covers roofs, but also a creative artist whose name is not proscribed, and who lends it to others whose names are proscribed. However, a piece of work signed by a *pokrývač* didn't give either side proper satisfaction. In the event of success, neither the owner of the name nor the real author could fully enjoy it.

The former pretended to be pleased about work that wasn't his, and the latter couldn't accept the acclaim.

The woman sitting next to Věra S. is her neighbor, and the visitor from Poland is standing.

Trying to fool the enemy didn't work. Anyone who calls Mrs. S.'s number from the phone book, and is lucky enough to have someone pick up at the thirty-fourth attempt, will find out that it's her grandson's number. Her grandson will give them a different number, at which nobody ever picks up the phone. If, a year later, they succeed in calling the grandson again, he will say he's terribly sorry, but he got two of the figures in his grandmother's phone number mixed up, he can't think why. So what if he gives them a new one? The number with the right figures is never answered either. The colleague who sent me to Kafka's niece because he's writing a book about people in Kafka's circle* had spoken to the son of another of Kafka's sisters. The son lives in Great Britain and asked him to send an e-mail, but gave him the wrong address, so the message came back a couple of times. Through trial and error, my colleague found the right address. He sent various questions, to which Kafka's nephew replied: "Please expect to receive an answer in the next fourteen days." And broke off the correspondence.

So the only advice I can give about the niece in Prague is that the visitor must stand at the gate of her house in person.

* I visited Věra S. at the request of Remigiusz Grzela. His book, *Bagaże Franza K.* ("Franz K.'s Luggage"), (Warsaw, 2004), was my source of information about Ottla David.

But there is never anybody named "S" at home.

You need luck, and thus you need to think of pressing the doorbell of the neighbors below to make inquiries. And then, unexpectedly, she is the one who answers what is apparently somebody else's intercom: "In this situation I'm not going to pretend I'm not here."

And so Věra S. is sitting in the spacious hall. At a round wooden table with no cloth, between blank white walls.

"Please explain to Mrs. S. what has brought you here," the neighbor begins.

"My colleague would very much like to have a conversation with Mrs. S., and I am his emissary. He has been trying to call you with no luck for two years."

Now Věra S. replies in a gentle tone: "Please ask your friend to send me a letter with his questions. I shall reply within a suitable time-frame."

I shift from foot to foot.

"Is there anything else I can do for you?" she says.

"It's a pity I can't ask you any questions myself," I admit regretfully.

"What question would you have for me?"

"Well, for instance—how do you feel in the twenty-first century?"

"Please send me a letter about it. I shall reply within a suitable time-frame."

LITTLE DARLING

It was getting harder and harder to bury someone. Suddenly burial had become unbelievably complicated.

Some people couldn't be buried at all. Josef S.'s family kept his urn at home. They had made several attempts to bury it, none of which had succeeded. Someone came up with the idea of doing it abroad, but the urn was unmasked in the express train to Vienna. It had been badly hidden in the restroom, between the toilet bowl and the wash basin.

Those who could be interred were also allowed to have their death announced in the newspaper, on one condition: the time of the funeral was not to be given.

Those who were allowed to publish the time only seemed to be better off. In fact, they were complicating the lives of their friends and acquaintances. This was lucidly explained by Reiner Kunze, a German poet who lived in Czechoslovakia:

A. has died. The funeral will be at five p.m., at the Motol crematorium. Those who live in Motol set off by four p.m. They know that if somebody like A. has died, it is not advisable for everybody to leave the house at the same time. To those who live further away it is obvious that they will be late, whatever time they set off. Because the streets will be closed, and the mourners' cars will be diverted through the suburbs and neighboring villages.

*Of course the only people who know about the fu-
neral are those whom there has been time to inform, because as soon as he died, the dead man's family's phones
stopped working. His relatives use public phone booths.
But the booths around their homes are out of order, so
they drive to booths in other districts. In practice, no-
tifying people is reduced to an anonymous informer
whispering into the receiver: "Funeral today at five p.m."*

Although not all funerals took place at such appealing
times of day. Not only was notice of the cremation of a certain biologist, a member of the Academy of Sciences, given
at the last moment, the information also came with the cruel
twist that it would be at 6:30 a.m. A famous philosopher was
cremated at 7 a.m., and there was no possibility of changing
the time.

A large number of funerals were set for the evening. When
the mourners came out of the crematorium, they would be
unable to see anything. The cemetery lighting would have
been switched off. However, Reiner Kunze noticed there was
an established custom that, if darkness had fallen, and the
road was on a slope, with occasional steps, anyone who came
to a step would stop and say: watch out, there's a step. And
nobody ever fell over.

MR. VÝBORNÝ

The cemetery in the Motol district is like a country graveyard:
small and cozy. It lies on a hill, among the trees, and when you
turn your back on the small chapel, you can easily forget there

is a city with a population of one and a half million stretched out below.

The manager of the cemetery and the gravedigger all in one was in the middle of his supper when a man and three women knocked at the door of his tiny cottage, not much bigger than a tomb. It was dark. He must have been surprised: who comes to look for a grave plot at that time of night?

"I've been all over the city and there's nowhere for me to bury my husband," said the older woman.

They looked tired. Since morning, they had been to every cemetery in the city, and everywhere they had been told that no more deceased were being accepted.

The gravedigger gave them a suspicious glance. "How come you've been all over the city?"

They didn't answer.

The dog began to growl, as if it could sense the tension.

"What exactly did he die of?" asked the gravedigger, surprised by their silence. ("We were as silent as children who've been up to no good," one of the two younger women recalls today.)

The man who was with the women took a sheet of paper from his pocket. The gravedigger looked at it. He read the diagnosis, the patient's age (forty-two), shifted his gaze to the printed letters of the surname, and then he knew. He sucked in air with a hiss. "I'm truly sorry," he said, handing back the sheet of paper. "My cemetery is full to bursting . . ."

"O God, that's the eighth cemetery now," said one of the women.

He looked at her and said: ". . . but I do have one grave here. For myself."

He picked up a flashlight and whistled for the dog. "Come on. I'll show you what a lovely plot I've got. Under a tree. There are some very decent people buried around it. My name is Výborný [meaning 'excellent'], so I couldn't pick anything ugly for myself."

The older woman cheered up distinctly, and tried to forestall his questions: "Of course I promise we won't bury him in the daytime. And at night the funeral won't bother anyone."

They reached the site of Mr. Výborný's grave.

"Lovely, isn't it?" he asked proudly. "Not even your husband could have chosen a better plot for himself," he said to the older woman. "Do you want it?"

"Very much," she replied. "But what . . . what will you do then?"

"I'll manage somehow. They always have to find a plot for the gravedigger. That's the only good thing about this sad trade."

"Writing isn't a very cheerful trade either," observed the man.

DIAGNOSIS

The diagnosis was bowel cancer. The deceased hadn't suspected it. In fact, he had been convinced he didn't have cancer at all.

All his life he had been particularly afraid of cancer, so when he had a gall bladder operation, he asked the doctors to examine his entire body to make sure there were no signs of it.

They did, and there weren't any. He was in the best hospital in the country, they couldn't possibly have got it wrong, his family thinks. The illness came along a month later.

He'd gone about the house in an elated mood saying: "I don't have cancer!"

Exactly eleven months before his death, on March 21, 1970, he was very happy. He had read in the newspaper that a program about him was being shown on television that evening. He called his friends and said: "There's a show about me tonight." The only thing he didn't ask himself was: Who made the program and why didn't he know about it before then? But he liked the idea that perhaps it was a surprise jubilee celebration of his creative work. After all, he was adored. In his country, they used the phrase "the people's little darling." And he knew he was one of the people's little darlings.

The TV schedule gave only the program title: *Report from on the Seine: About Writer and Screenwriter Jan Procházka*.

CHAMPAGNE

They bought champagne and his wife made some fancy sandwiches. "The bottle's on ice," he joyfully told a friend over the phone. "It's all very nice, and what's more, just imagine, I haven't got cancer," he joked. He and his wife and three daughters settled down in front of the set. It was the so-called peak viewing time.

An hour later the program ended.

The champagne stood untouched in warm water.

No one had eaten a single sandwich, and next morning their daughter threw them in the trash can.

Jan Procházka sat dumbly in front of the television, staring at the switched-off screen. Somebody had eavesdropped on his private conversations with a friend, recorded them, and broadcast them on TV.

Nobody said a word except the confused writer who kept repeating the same words: "That was my voice . . . it really was my voice, but . . . but I didn't say that."

The first call came through, and his wife picked it up. A man wanted to speak to Mr. Procházka urgently. "You despicable swine," he began. "At last we know who you really are."

"You're a monstrous, shameless, two-faced bastard. One for show, the other at home," the writer learned from the next call.

It must have been then—says his daughter Lenka—that his crushed spirit sent his body a signal, and the irreversible process began.

Her younger sister, Iva, thought it was the worst day of their lives, but she was wrong.

Next day, the radio began to broadcast the secretly taped private conversations of Jan Procházka, in seven episodes over fourteen days.

With one day's delay, the country's biggest newspaper published them in print.

A WRITER'S HAPPINESS

He became the people's little darling during the Spring.

It was a spring that had been prepared for the previous summer. In June 1967, the Writers Union had held a congress. The opening speech was made by the ruling Communist Party secretary for culture: "At a moment like this," he said, "we should strengthen our alliance with the Soviet Union."

He also expressed his expectations: "The Party expects you to formulate criteria for socialist literature."

Despite the fact that Stalin was long since dead, the writers were yet again supposed to be making a public statement about the role of art—that it's not about love, but about class struggle.

Nobody could have anticipated what happened next.

The first speaker was an author of novels and socialist-realist poetry, which he even went on writing after Stalin's death, who had joined the Party when he was still in high school.

Suddenly, as if against his better judgment, he read out a quotation from a letter written by Voltaire to Hevelius: "I do not agree with what you are saying, but I shall defend to the death your right to be able to say it freely." "That's a wonderful remark," said the Party writer to his colleagues, "it is the fundamental ethical principle of modern culture. Anyone who wishes to go back to the days before this principle is regressing to the Middle Ages." (It was Milan Kundera.)

The audience—as witnesses recall—was dumbstruck, and the bald Party secretary who had demanded the alliance of literature with the USSR clenched his lips tight.

Photographs taken at the congress show more than forty writers sitting along tables in their shirtsleeves. They have taken off their jackets and are gesticulating.

At the very end, on the third day, the son of a peasant from Moravia took the floor; a farmer by education, he was an eminent screenwriter and member of the ideological board of the Czechoslovak Communist Party's Central Committee, and his name was Jan Procházka. He had such faith in communism that, shocked by his views, his parents hadn't attended his own wedding. He had written a lot, but the critics had judged his first screenplays to be lackluster. For eight years, he had been a full-time screenwriter at the Barrandov Film Studios. There he underwent a creative metamorphosis. He discovered that not every screenplay has to be educational, and that what kills creativity is sticking to a formula. For a decade, only one of his movies had been produced each year, occasionally two. They were usually directed by Karel Kachyňa, one of the founders of the new wave in Czechoslovak cinema, who was Polish director Agnieszka Holland's tutor at the Prague film school. "At the very same moment," said Procházka, "the writer is happy with those who are happy, and desperate with those who are desperate."

A murmur ran through the room.

No other member of the Central Committee was as brilliant, not even those who were involved in literature.

"We are brothers to all those who love, because our main weapon is the heart," he added.

According to historians, the Party secretary left the congress hissing: "You're going to muck it all up . . ." However, those present in the auditorium claim that the secretary had said something similar, but put in a different way:

"You're going to fuck it all up," he said.

SPRING, CONTINUED

That was how the ferment began, which culminated in the aforementioned Spring. The congress of writers and poets came out in opposition to the Party. The system's own gravediggers had evolved from within.

"In the Czechoslovak Communist Party, there was a large number of decent people who were horrified by what they had set their hands to"—thirty years later, so said the man who explained to Mr. Výborný at the cemetery that writing is just as sad as burying the dead.

(It was Pavel Kohout. He must have had himself in mind too. He had written his final poem praising the regime after Stalin's death: "He is not dead! He is just asleep / He will be here forever, within you and within me.")

Europe couldn't believe its eyes and ears: here was a communist party that had managed to regain the support of a significant part of society without applying force.

Six months after the writers' congress, the First Secretary of the Communist Party, who was also the state president, was removed from his post. He was Antonín Novotný—a gloomy, solemn man. It was his conviction that anything that did not fall within the Soviet model was not socialism. In January 1968, he was replaced within the Party by Alexander Dubček, who allowed the public to speak freely and to photograph each other in nothing but their bathing suits at the pool.

People stopped being afraid of each other, and society was full of admiration for itself.

A sort of miracle had occurred.

The newspapers and television lost their colorlessness. The tedium vanished from the theater and cinema. Banned books were published. Censorship was lifted.

In a cartoon in the previously regime-run newspaper *Rudé právo*, one guy says to another at a café table: "There's nothing to talk about. It's all in the papers."

In another cartoon, a young couple are standing under a

tree. The man is carving a large heart into the bark, with the name "DUBČEK" inside it.

People even painted slogans on the walls in Poland, such as: "All Poland is waiting for its Dubček."

HURRAY!

Thirty-nine-year-old Procházka wrote newspaper columns and had daily meetings with young people. In those days, some of them were even held in the city parks.

"Not everyone can be a philosopher, but in his own interest each person should devote half an hour a week to thinking," he advised in his book *Politics for Everyone*. It was an instant bestseller. He received up to fifty letters a day, because he knew how to explain various problems.

"Is it at all possible to be happy these days?" he was asked. Or: "Why are the reviewers comparing the Czech movie *The Hop Pickers* to *West Side Story*, when the ordinary citizen still can't see this American movie, although it came out six years ago? Can you confirm that our comrades from the Central Committee watch American movies in secret?"

"They accuse us of attacking socialism," he told the young people. "But those charges are brought by the very men and women who have made socialism into a dreary prison for the intellect." ("He was like the first Christians," adds his daughter. "He believed that socialism is the best system. My son is convinced that the ideas his grandfather promoted in those days could still be a success. But I always say they'd have to be implemented by angels.")

In March 1968, at a meeting held at the Slavonic House in

Prague, he uttered a famous remark about censorship: "Man did not spend ages learning to talk only to end up with no right to speak."

"Hurray!" the crowd of students cried in answer.

"Some historians believe to this day that the main aim of the Soviet invasion was to destroy freedom of speech in our country," wrote Dubček in 1990.

"We're not afraid of scary monsters anymore," declared Procházka. "A return to democracy does not have to mean a return to capitalism."

And also: "Let's not teach cows to fly; if we're going to try at all, let's teach the horses. They're more than twice as intelligent."

HANDS

Let's go back to the evening of March 21, 1970.

First, the TV viewers saw an Air France plane landing at an airport.

Then, a terminal building marked PARIS.

"Paris is a beautiful city, full of cultural monuments. But not all of us go there to admire them," said a straight-talking female voice.

After the terminal, they saw the interior of a car, and a pair of hands. White shirt cuffs protruded from the sleeves of a coat. The hands were driving a Mercedes. The right one occasionally held a cigarette, tapping the ash into an ashtray on the dashboard.

The only performers in the movie *Report from on the Seine* were these two hands.

Off went the car. A road was visible through the front windshield. According to the woman's voice, it was meant to be the highway from the airport into Paris, but it looked like the highway from Prague to Karlovy Vary in western Bohemia.

The invisible owner of the hands was talking to another— also invisible—person.

It is certain that one of the voices in the car belonged to the writer Jan Procházka. This is what he said: "On Saturday I had a meeting with some people from the government. They're cretins. And Dubček isn't any smarter either."

"Uh-huh," said the other voice.

"The man has good intentions, but he has obvious limitations . . . He's not the sort of person who could possibly manage to do anything except keep adapting to the situation."

"Yes, but . . ." added the voice.

"In which case he should wave goodbye to the top job in the Party. Because it's idiotic."

"Uh-huh."

"They've got to find the key to it all! Ways to deal with all those stupid cleaners or lunch ladies who appear up there with the help of those equally stupid Party secretaries."

"Yes, too true," confirmed the voice.

THE VOICE

The "uh-huh" and other affirmations came from a well-known professor of literature whom the writer had met two years earlier. They had talked for four hours as they drank a bottle of vodka. The recording came from this particular conversation.

They had never been to Paris together. They had never been on a car journey together. The Mercedes didn't belong to either the professor or the writer. Procházka didn't have a car or a driver's license. Even though the noise of an engine had been added over their voices, an echo could be heard, which doesn't happen when you're in a car. It's easy to tell they were talking somewhere else, in a place with tiling on the walls, for example.

And, in actual fact, the source of the echo was the professor's tiled kitchen.

"Why exactly are we showing this?" asked the voice-over. "To give you the chance to form your own opinion about the democratic spirit in which those whom you were so eager to believe talk to each other."

When some "pissed-off miners from Ostrava" called his house, Procházka spent a long time explaining to them that those were his words, but not his opinions. (We know this because there are instructions in the Security Service archives, declassified in March 2001, setting out who was to call Procházka and what they were to say. We know how these tasks went.)

His wife unplugged the phone.

"How pale you are," she said to the Person Under Surveillance. The PUS made no reply.

THE HOOK

They couldn't sleep.

Suddenly, at four in the morning, they heard the crash of breaking glass.

They ran into the sitting room.

A large mirror had fallen from the wall and shattered against the floor.

Only the hook was still there, high up on the wall.

The writer stared at the hook, then at his wife, and asked what it could mean. She didn't reply.

Their daughter Lenka says the mirror couldn't withstand the tension in the apartment, where six people were lying awake, suffering.

THE BALCONY

For a long time, he refused to believe a recording could be manipulated to quite that extent. "He was a screenwriter, his movies had won prizes. I realize he didn't edit them, but he must have known what could be done with a tape," I wonder out loud.

"No, he couldn't have understood that. He really was just a naive boy from the countryside," says his wife, Mahulena.

He stopped leaving the house.

The nation believed the television.

Kundera wrote that plenty of people who bitch about their own friends at the first opportunity were more shocked by their beloved Procházka than by the methods of the secret police.

For two weeks, he paced up and down the balcony.

If he did any whispering to himself out there, he could be heard—unbeknown to him—by nine microphones.

Fourteen days after the program was broadcast, he fell ill with a temperature of 42 degrees C [107°F].

He sat and wrote. He typed out hundreds of letters of explanation. To the editors of newspapers, to the radio and television stations. None of them was ever published. So he sent
explanations to his barber and to the manager of his favorite
Chinese restaurant.

At college, nobody would speak to Lenka—she was the
daughter of the man who had betrayed the Spring. So she
brought in twenty copies of her father's letter, and tried to
get her fellow students to read his explanations. Her younger
sister Iva took copies to high school too.

But their classmates said: "Don't give us that letter."

"Don't destroy people."

"Why would you even touch those pieces of paper?"

NAIVETY

TV director and documentary filmmaker Jordi Niubó listened carefully to the soundtrack of *Report from on the Seine*
through headphones (the audibility is much better than without), and today, thirty years on, he is convinced Procházka's
words haven't been transposed. "He really did say Dubček
was naive, etcetera. But he was, wasn't he? Today anyone will
agree that he was. But at the time it sounded like real sacrilege
in Czechoslovakia."

Years later, Dubček himself frankly admitted to having
been misled by his own imagination: "The problem for me
was that I didn't have a crystal ball to help me see the invasion coming."

At 11 p.m. on August 20, 1968, the Russians attacked
Prague from the air. The airplanes dropped tanks and guns

at Prague airport. At dawn, before the Soviets seized Dubček and five other people in charge of the country, seven Soviet paratroopers entered his office. "Immediately," he recalls, "they took up position by the windows and internal doors. It looked like an armed robbery. I automatically reached for the phone, but one of the soldiers pointed his machine gun at me, grabbed the phone, and ripped the cable from the wall."

They sat Dubček and the others at a large table. Next to him sat his friend, the chairman of parliament Josef Smrkovský (the man whose urn would be discovered on the express train to Vienna five years later). "Indeed," writes Dubček, "we were pretty well protected as we sat around the table—each of us had a machine-gun barrel aimed at the back of his head." As they were leaving, he noticed a man called So-ják, the head of his chancellery. "I whispered to him to keep an eye on my briefcase, in which there were some official documents: I didn't want them to fall into the hands of the Russians. At that point I didn't know Soják was one of the Soviet lackeys."

Abducted and imprisoned by the Russians ("At the Kremlin I was not allowed to wash off the dust and dirt of the last three days"), he knew his country had been invaded by a gigantic military machine, and that there was no force on earth capable of driving it out. Nevertheless, as he recalls, it was only when he was sitting in front of Brezhnev, with no doubt left in his mind that he had to sign the—forcibly imposed— act of capitulation, that he realized the most important thing: "that in this madhouse nothing made sense—none of the ideals to which I was attached, and which I had thought both sides shared."

Wasn't he naive?

Right up to that moment, he had believed those people had ideals!

PACKAGES

By the time the Procházka family were sitting in front of the TV set looking forward to the special program, Alexander Dubček was no longer First Secretary of the Communist Party, but ambassador to Turkey. (Three months later, he was an employee of the State Forestry Service in Slovakia.) The First Secretary was now Gustav Husák.

The professor responsible for the "uh-huhs" and other affirmative noises in *Report from on the Seine* was historian of literature Václav Černý. He was twenty-six years old when, in 1931, he became an associate professor at the University of Geneva. He discovered some unknown plays by Pedro Calderón, and was quickly acclaimed as one of the most outstanding representatives of Czech culture in the twentieth century. An inveterate opponent of communism, he was the target of propaganda campaigns from the Stalinist era until his death in 1987. If he took an interest in the Middle Ages, he was attacked for being partial to an age of ignorance; if he turned to the Baroque, he was accused of doing it out of admiration for the Jesuits; and if he wrote about Romanticism, he was charged with being an individualist, which disqualifies a citizen from being a true socialist. Whereas he was only interested in Iberian studies out of reverence for General Franco. After the Prague Spring, he was forced to retire, and his work was only issued by émigré publishers.

The makers of the provocative television show had deliberately not revealed too many of his words. His other recorded remarks were needed for a series of radio programs,
entitled *On Professor Černý and Others*. The others, bugged at
Černý's house, were Procházka, Havel and Kohout.

"The wheels have begun to turn," ran the title of the first
program.

They described how the tapes of the conversations had
reached the media: "History has many remarkable stories
about how things that should have been kept hidden forever
suddenly came to light."

And they went on: "In this instance, some packages just
as suddenly appeared on the desks of the managers of the
mass media. The sender was anonymous, but the postmark
implied that they came from the city on the Seine. However,
despite that country's reputation, the packages didn't contain
bottles of cognac, but tape recordings. On them, we heard
some voices familiar to us from the Prague Spring."

On the tapes, Václav Havel talked about the possibility of
creating a social democracy similar to the Swedish model. He
said he could see Professor Černý taking part in it.

The professor told Procházka one-to-one that he wasn't
backing out, "but first Dubček has to win. For himself, not for
me. For himself! Once he wins, I'll show my face. If necessary,
I'll even come out against Dubček."

"A shiver goes down the spine," wrote a commentator,
"when we hear how cynically they traded the fate of the
country and its people, with no embarrassment or shame."
And he concluded: "We realize that the bourgeois media
are bound to create complex rhetorical constructs around

our series—we're already familiar with that sort of hysterical outcry. But the tapes could not remain hidden. Once upon a time, these voices spoke words that were like honey for the people's hearts. But in private they didn't conceal their hatred for our world."

As for the bourgeois media, according to *Süddeutsche Zeitung*, for example, Prague was already experiencing George Orwell's *1984* in 1970.

OLD PEOPLE'S HOME

Not long ago, Jordi Niubó endeavored to find out where the people who signed their names to those productions are today. The documentation for *Report from on the Seine* has disappeared, and there's nothing left in the television file but the wire binding.

The people listed in the program's closing titles are either not alive anymore, or nobody knows anything about them. The man who was head of Prague television in 1970 stopped working there in the mid-1980s, and it is impossible to establish where he lives now. According to the newspaper *Rudé právo*, they obtained the recording from radio broadcasts made by someone called Karel Janík. It praised the editor for doing a good job. No such person ever existed. Karel Janík is the secret police.

The man who was Minister for Internal Affairs in those days is still alive. Niubó saw his hunched back in an old people's home. "He might mistake you for his mother," the nurse warned him.

THE EAR

It is the late 1950s.

Ludvik, secretary to a certain government minister, and his wife Anna are on their way home from a party. At their front gate, it turns out they've lost their keys, so they break into their own home.

The keys are there, stuck in the lock, but on the inside. But they had locked the door behind them—Ludvik had had the keys in his pocket.

Somebody has switched off the electricity. Anna is drunk, and criticizes her husband for not even knowing how to mend a fuse; they start bickering about stupid things, they tussle, and suddenly a fork falls to the kitchen floor. It has fallen between two cabinets. Anna insists on getting it out of there. In the narrow gap between the cabinets, she finds an "ear."

Ludvik panics, and starts burning all his compromising documents. He throws them into the toilet bowl and tries to flush them away. The bathroom is filled with acrid smoke, but they're afraid to open a window. They've noticed that there are two men sitting in a car, watching their property.

They find another "ear" in the bathroom under the dirty laundry.

The next one is close to the ceiling, on the sill of the little bathroom window.

(After the Soviet invasion, Procházka wrote a short story about an "ear." It was soon filmed by a friend of his as *The Ear*.

(An "ear" is a tiny chip with an antenna the length of an eyelash. A transmitter.)

Ludvik realizes that his minister, who lives across the street, has been interned in his own home. What's the meaning of the lack of electricity in Ludvik's villa and the three bugging devices they've found? They're sure to be coming for him as well. Anna sorts out some shirts for her husband, and gets him ready for arrest.

Once our hero has revealed his fear, cowardice and lack of character to the audience, the next morning he is not arrested, but appointed minister.

TABOO

The Ear immediately became legendary and was marked down for deletion. There was only one copy of the movie, which was known as "detained production No. 1." It was described as one of the best movies in the history of Czech cinema, and definitely the best ever made by director Karel Kachyňa.

The movie remained in detention for twenty years.

An "ear"—the personification of an invisible being. A complement to Kafka's ideas. Everyone knows it's listening all the time, but they can't talk about it, not even in a whisper; only Anna, through stupidity and to spite her husband, lets herself go round the house shouting: "An ear . . . A goddamn ear!" In Procházka's novella, the "ear" is a sacred kind of symbol. "It becomes a sort of god, whose name no one dares to utter," said one of the reviews.

Procházka never suspected that he himself was being bugged and recorded in the first days of the Prague Spring, after Dubček came to power. He thought they had only started to do it after the Soviet invasion.

Meanwhile, Dubček himself had been presented with a

technological novelty: the prototype of the first Czechoslovak color TV, to try out at home. When he realized there was a bugging device in the TV set, he stopped using it, took it down to the cellar, and deliberately didn't tell anyone about it. Two weeks later, the man who had given him the TV set questioned him in person: "So tell me, aren't you watching color TV anymore, comrade?"

LOVE

In 1968, Procházka's daughter Lenka was seventeen. She has been in love many times since then. In January 2001, when further Security Service documents were declassified, she found out that three of her boyfriends had been recruited by the secret police, and had made regular reports on their relationship.

"Do you feel hatred towards them?"

"I was shocked, I'll admit. But I'm not going to let some new piece of information ruin my memories of a relationship. Because what is the truth? The truth is what we experienced, not what someone's going to tell us about it years later.

"I feel sorry for those guys. They were a part of my life. If I'd blocked off my emotions, if I hadn't smiled at one of them in the metro, if they hadn't come into my life, they wouldn't have had any problems, and the Security Service would never have offered them the temptation that they did.

"Yes, they weren't brave. But they had other virtues.

"You can't measure everyone by your own yardstick.

"For the people I have loved I have a different yardstick."

THE BLONDE

When the children were little, she went off to the swimming pool. There, she met a nice girl. With fair hair, always smiling. They became friends. For several years, the blonde girl took care of her children, did the cooking, and stayed the night. "All my life, I was sure it was I who had picked her out of the crowd, I who had approached her, I who had offered her a cup of coffee," she says. "And now from the files I've learned that she was a secret police operative placed at the pool. She made copies of all the letters she found in my apartment."

A CLOSE FRIEND

Everyone who remembers this episode instructs me: "But don't forget to write that when Procházka was dying Kachyňa played the dirtiest trick on him—before his death, he gave an interview saying that he regretted everything they had filmed together."

Karel Kachyňa was a close friend of Procházka. At his interrogation, the security officers demanded that he distance himself from the movies they had made together. Especially *The Ear*. That was the condition imposed on him by the state. He must disown Procházka, and then he would be able to go on working.

The interview in question appeared in the cinema journal *Zábĕr* (meaning "The Take"), and on the same day *Rudé právo* reprinted extracts from it along with a commentary. However, it was two months after Jan's death, a fact nobody remembers, but then who'd want to go through the papers from thirty years ago?

Not once does Procházka's name appear in either article. Kachyňa talks about his new movie. As for settling scores, all he says is: "Nobody is infallible. Least of all me, since I work on emotional topics."

The journalist presses him: "But perhaps you could say a bit more about that?"

Kachyňa: "It would be easy here, on paper, to disown everything that belongs to yesterday, while ardently signing one's name to everything that belongs to today."

And that's just about all he says. One more sentence about socialism and a promise to make a movie about Lenin in the future.

"Karel Kachyňa's words are to be warmly welcomed, as they imply that he is now on the right path towards self-awareness," wrote the *Rudé právo* commentator.

From then on, Kachyňa made movies for children, and never produced anything about Lenin.

THE MORGUE

Nowadays, Karel Kachyňa lives* near Prague Castle, in a pleasant house with a small garden. He is seventy-six. As I

---

* Karel Kachyňa died on March 12, 2004, two years after this essay was originally published in Poland. Besides *The Ear*, Kachyňa and Procházka's most important co-production is *Coach to Vienna* (1966), one of the most controversial movies of that era. The heroine is a desperate village woman whose husband has been hanged by the Germans. On the final day of the war, a young Nazi soldier forces her to transport him and his wounded comrade by horse and cart across the border illegally. The woman takes a sickle with her, in order to kill them both at the first opportunity. However, first a mutual liking arises between the young German and the woman, and then desire. At this point, they are attacked by Czech partisans. The movie was criticized as anti-Czech. Procházka and Kachyňa explained that it was "simply a movie against killing."

am on my way to see him one sunny February morning, I think about fate. In a period of about fifteen years, four of his screenwriters and script originators died. First Procházka, then two years later the writer Ota Pavel—a sports journalist who saw the Devil, ended up in the hospital as a result, and started to write as part of his therapy. Kachyňa adapted his memoir *The Death of the Beautiful Deer* for the screen. Then two more of them died.

"My house is a former morgue converted into an apartment," a small, skinny, wrinkled man tells me on the threshold. "But there aren't any ghosts, because if there were, the dogs would refuse to live here," he reassures me.

We bring up the interview.

"I had to give it, or for twenty years I wouldn't have been able to make any movies, and I'm a born filmmaker," he explains. "So the journalist and I spent a month working on that little bit of text. You see this sentence about socialism, right here?"

"Yes."

"To avoid saying that I was going to support socialism, the editor and I thought up the following phrase: 'I am convinced that most artists who live in this country want to serve the idea of socialism; each of them wants to be a faithful mirror of modern times and a sensitive detector of the future.'

"I didn't say 'I am in favor of socialism,' I just said that others 'are in favor.' Now you can see that what people think is true nowadays is stronger than what really happened. The commentary in *Rudé právo* made an impression on people, and now they've got it all mixed up together, my carefully considered words and the communist propaganda," says the director, staring into space.

I think I can sense the right moment. "Let's talk about Procházka," I suggest.

"I can't," he replies. "As soon as I talk about him, I sink into a dreadful depression. So I try to say as little as possible about him."

Our conversation can go no further.

As a way of making up for the awkward silence, the old man suddenly fetches the screenplay of *The Ear* out of a drawer.

He asks if I'd like to hold it. He says it's the original director's copy with hand-written corrections. I pick up a fat typescript on blue paper.

FEVER

This is the land of Kafka. "In a political trial the fact of the defendant's birth is already a crime in itself."

This is the only complaint against fate that Professor Černý wrote in his 1,600-page diary. By contrast with Procházka, he was steady as a rock, according to his friends.

Whereas the writer had been lying in the hospital for the past ten months. His trial was under preparation, and the secret police were taking an interest in his illness.

("4.02.1971, the PUS had a fever of 39˚ C [102˚ F].")

When a friend came to visit him, Mrs. Procházková asked the visitor not to show any signs of shock. "Jan looks terrible," she said. "We're expecting the end any day now."

"And one more thing," she added. "He doesn't know he's got cancer."

"You have to know how to fight a fever," he began as soon as he saw his friend in the doorway. He talked for half an hour without stopping. "By now I can tell when it's coming over me. If I were to give in and fall asleep after dinner, I'd wake up in an hour or so with a raging fever. It's as if it's just waiting for me to lie down and wilt. But I won't! I walk about, stand up, sit down, go to the bathroom, look out of the window, wait for the right time when I have to take one drug or another, then the doctor comes, then my wife, she cooks for me and brings in the food afterwards, so I have to eat it, because I've no business losing strength over things that are bound to happen. And so evening comes. And the temperature I get at night is no longer quite so high. Then I sleep two hours, I get up, walk about, stand still, sit, take a look out of the window, over and over, and fall asleep at dawn. Then the day comes and the whole thing repeats itself. I've got to be on the offensive all the time and never give in!"

The offensive lasted thirteen days longer.

The doctors decided on another bowel operation.

During the operation, the power station cut off the electricity for forty-five minutes. So they operated on him with the help of flashlights and candles.

THE LAMB

In 2000, Lenka Procházková's popular novel about the life of Jesus was published, *The Lamb*. As in the Apocrypha, the author had to create scenes to fill in the gaps in the basic story offered by the Gospels, and she had to invent the dialogues.

It was a while before she realized where she had gotten the words Mary addresses to Jesus when He is brought down from the cross.

They were the words her mother used to say goodbye to her father on his hospital bed.

"All the bad things have already happened. I know how much they have wronged you. But you are no longer in pain. Only I am in pain."

A PARTLY OPEN DOOR

The head of Czechoslovak cinematography publicly criticized himself on television for having been too close to Jan Procházka.

He burst into tears in front of the cameras and said the writer had disappointed him.

Then he came to see Iva, Lenka and Mahulena and said: "They interrogated me at the police station and I heard him. I heard your Jan from behind a partly open door! But I knew he was dying in the hospital. And at that point I thought: 'Oh my God, they even interrogate dying people.' And I was terrified about what would happen to me.

"It never even crossed my mind that they were playing me a taped voice from the other room."

LIFE, CONTINUED

Pavel Kohout, who three days earlier had pointed out to Mr. Výborný the similarity between the work of a writer and a gravedigger, made a speech over the coffin.

Nowadays, he says that funeral was the symbolic end of the Prague Spring and the beginning of winter. Most of Procházka's former friends didn't come. By the same token, the Czech cultural elite were divided into the vast majority, who surrendered, and a microscopic minority, who seven years later became the group of "pretenders and castaways from Charter 77," as the press called them.

Kohout also says that many artists felt relieved as, day by day, they gradually found out about the Procházka affair. Thanks to those lousy programs, they were able to say: "We're not going to associate with people like him anymore." And the story confirmed their belief that one should comply with the regime after all—that made life easier.

Kohout later emigrated to Austria, where he wrote a novel about a girl who hadn't gotten into theater school, so she began training to be an executioner. At the school for executioners, she realized that just about anyone can hang a person, but the art is to hang them in such a way as to contain in this act the entire history of human civilization, right up to the technological revolution.

When, in the fall of 1979, he tried to go back to Prague, he was forced out of his car on the Czechoslovak border and deported to Austria. Straight after that, the authorities stripped him of his Czechoslovak citizenship.

Výborný the gravedigger died ten years after Procházka. He didn't end up in an equally beautiful spot. He was buried on the sidelines, closer to the cemetery wall. He was put in a communal grave, where he lies along with strangers.

Lenka was expelled from college, and for twelve years she worked as a cleaner.

Iva, who graduated from high school, was denied the right to go to college. She was given a job at the airport, packing dinners for passengers into plastic compartments on trays.

All their father's books were withdrawn from circulation. Kohout wrote that Procházka, like many others, was "silenced to death."

PEACE

Ninety days after the funeral, in May 1971, the Czechoslovak Communist Party Congress was held, which opened with the words: "We have conquered chaos."

It was the president of the republic who was speaking. "For the past two years," he said, "the Central Committee under the leadership of comrade Husák has accomplished a task worthy of respect."

In the name of the artists, actress Jiřina Švorcová, who played the store assistant in the TV series *A Woman Behind the Counter*, sighed with relief at the lectern: "At last!"

"In 1968," she continued, "the enemies of socialism unleashed the problem of so-called 'absolute freedom of artistic creativity.' Backed by the applause of the West, eventually they began to inspire in people a lack of faith in socialism as the basic principle of life."

A SLIP OF PAPER

As I hold the fat script of *The Ear* in front of me, director Karel Kachyňa is encouraging me to leaf through it, when a slip of paper falls from inside.

"Oh, that's Procházka's writing. Take a look, I think he wrote something about *The Ear* there," he says.

Yes, he did.

"This story is made up. The things that really happened were far more terrible."

THE PUBLIC CONCERN

In 2000, reporters for *Blesk* ("Flash"), the post-communist Czech Republic's top-selling newspaper, wrote about singer Helena Vondráčková's jaw, pointing out which of her teeth were false.

In 2003, they gave the number of the courtroom where she was granted her divorce.

In 2004, they photographed and described every item of trash in her trash can.

In 2005, they published a list of plastic surgery procedures which she should—in their view—immediately undergo.

Among all these items, they also reported:

THE TRUTH ABOUT MY CHILD
VONDRÁČKOVÁ—AT LAST WE TELL ALL!

From our reporter, Prague—Deep inside, Helena Vondráčková (56) has suppressed a terrible secret for years on end. Finally it has come to light. If not for the bungled termination which her one-time German lover forced her to undergo, Helena would now have an adult son or daughter! Even though decades have gone by, time has never healed the wound. It still hurts to this day! Every time she sees a baby in a pram she starts to choke up.

When this dreadful thing happened, Helena's world crumbled. The lyricist Zdeněk Borovec wrote a song for her, "Two Little Wings Are Gone" [the Czech version of the American hit "Killing Me Softly"].

Search in every corner of the house
You won't find anything but shadows
Two little wings are gone now
They were almost here
Where have they flown to, where are they now
The nest is empty
The heart is silent

. . . Yes, this song is about her! It's a poem about a tragedy . . .

For years we've been hearing rumors about Helena—that she was never interested in having children, that instead of being a mother she preferred to have a career and to earn millions as a singer, and that she didn't want pregnancy to ruin her perfect figure. But all that was just hot air! She alone knew the truth. And for all these years she has kept her silence . . .

Something terrible happened!

At the time, she was on tour in America, where she had gone to sing for her compatriots. One day she felt unwell and the doctor declared: "Miss Vondráčková, you're going to be a mother!" She beamed all over. At last! She rushed to the phone to give the news to her lover, Helmut Sickel, who later became her first husband. But there was a cold shower in store for her. "A child? Now? You've gone crazy!" he sharply reined her in. "Helena, be sensible! I live in Germany, you live in Prague, there'd be problems. The child will have to be aborted!" She couldn't listen to any more. With tears in her eyes she hung up. Her heart was filled with despair, regret, and confusion. Helmut was the only man she loved that much! More than herself, more than her dreams. And so she did as he said.

And the doctor wrote a short
Official note
The first mention of someone
The final mention
You're no longer a mother, girl
The bird no longer sings

"To avoid exposing herself to accusations and condemnation she didn't go to a hospital. Unfortunately, she fell into the wrong hands, and then there was no question of ever becoming pregnant again," claims one of Helena's closest friends . . .

We also asked the older citizens of Slatiňany, Helena's home town, what they know about this affair. "It's a great mystery," say the locals. But not a word more. They don't want to open old wounds, they love their Helena too much for that . . .

There was no journalist's name below the article.

The issue of *Blesk* including "the truth about Helena" sold a record number of copies. Despite a court case that the interested party won against the newspaper, which had to pay her damages, the editors continue to regard Vondráčková as the people's darling, meaning that *Blesk* is entitled to reveal her personal life.

"In what way is that any different from the practices of the communist Security Service?" I ask.

"In every way!" says one of the journalists. "First of all, by contrast with the Security Service we aim to meet public expectations. Secondly, our publication has nothing to do with communism, because we're part of a Swiss capitalist concern."

LIFE IS LIKE A MAN

She came into the recording suite in a sheepskin coat.

It was November 14, 1989, quite a cold day. Communism would come to an end in a month's time. The face that appeared from behind the glasses, warm scarf and fur collar was not a familiar one.

She took off her coat and went into the studio. The sound director asked her to do a voice test.

He went pale, glanced at the movie director, and said: "Fero, you must be crazy!"

She began singing her warm-up exercises.

Over the past twenty years, her voice had become husky, deeper, but it was still her. "And unfortunately, they recognized her by it," says Fero Fenič. The assistant sound director grabbed his bag of sandwiches and the recording editor seized his briefcase. The cleaner grabbed her beret and said: "My child is sick!"

"They ran like the plague," the director recalls. "You have no idea what terrible terror they had in their eyes. Do you say 'terrible terror' in your language too? They fled the studio like rats," he adds.

The film *Strange Beings* is about the last night of communism. Fenič must have foreseen that night, because he started filming it in February 1989 but, as he says, out of fear no Czech actors were willing to play the leading roles, so the parts were played by Poles.

She sang the song for the closing credits.

Until 1970, Marta Kubišová is a pop star. She sings in a trio with Helena Vondráčková and Vaclav Neckář. After 1970, people cross the road at the sight of her.

In the photos taken at the MIDEM music fair held in Cannes in 1969, she is still happy. Neckář is holding her and Vondráčková tight around the waist, and it's clear that both girls are belting it out.

In a photo taken twenty-one years later, she is frightened. She looks like an office worker (a postwoman? a store assistant?) whom someone has told to get up on stage. She is glancing fearfully into the camera and has too many gray hairs.

But let's go back to the photos from Cannes.

A year, at most two years after Neckář held her and Helena round the waist, she should have appeared at a festival in Sopot, Poland. The three of them would have been a sensation, Sopot '70 would have gone wild with joy. "Vondráčková, Kubišová, and Neckář—the famous Czech trio, the Golden Kids, who conquered the Paris Olympia!" the presenter Lucjan Kydryński would have announced. From that moment on, Marta would have been as famous in Poland as Helena ended up being.

But that's not what happened.

On February 3, 1970, Neckář was summoned by the head of Pragokoncert, František Hrabal, who placed on the desk before him three pictures torn from a Danish magazine called *Hot Kittens*. "Take a good look at this, Mr. Neckář. One of these girls is Kubišová. You realize Pragokoncert can no longer work with an artist like that. If you want to go on tour, you and Vondráčková will be going alone."

"Forgive me, Mr. Hrabal. I have been working with Marta Kubišová for seven years, but I have never seen her in this sort of pose before. Perhaps if you were to call her husband . . ."

"We know you people! We are perfectly aware how you artists behave . . . I'll show you a porn movie that Kubišová made for a thousand West German marks in a villa in Prague! And then you'll recognize her."

He didn't show it to him.

The Golden Kids ceased to exist. *Rudé právo* wrote that Marta Kubišová had posed for some pornographic photos and could no longer be a socialist artist.

In the days when Czech art books had only black-and-white reproductions of van Gogh paintings, the Security Service was very good at faking Danish porn magazines, producing photographs in the very same colors, on exactly the same sort of paper, but with Marta's face.

Only a year earlier, the reviewers in Paris had written: "Marta, Helena, and Vašek are socialism with a human face." Josephine Baker was among those who praised them. But unfortunately, since then the twenty-eight-year-old Marta had infuriated the regime.

• • •

When the Soviet tanks entered the streets of Prague, Kubišová had just been asked to record the final song for a television serial, *Songs for Rudolph III*. The program told the story of a kingdom where the king's death is followed by chaos, but then along comes a knight who drives out the traitors and marries the princess. In Marta Kubišová's low voice, the princess sings:

> *May peace be with this land,*
> *May spite, envy, jealousy, strife, and terror*
> *be at an end, let them now be at an end.*

The program went out twice. The song, to words by Petro Rada, became an anthem. The radio, which was still controlled by the Prague Spring team, broadcast it as "A Prayer for Marta." People started singing it on the streets, among the Soviet tanks.

"To this day," says the writer Lenka Procházková, "some people weep when they hear the 'Prayer.' Just as I do."

The new head of Czech radio, appointed in the wake of the invasion, ruled that they should only broadcast one work by Kubišová daily. They had to weaken her position in the forthcoming popular vote for the Golden Nightingale award.

She had won it in 1968. The Golden Nightingale was the top prize a singer could win from the public. In the male category, it was always won by the tenor Karol Gott.

The votes were counted, and despite the efforts to damage her, Marta Kubišová still won the female vocalist category.

At that point, Edvard Švach, head of the censor's department and formerly a Stalinist prosecutor, paid a visit to the competition office and told them how the public vote should work. They should combine the male and female categories, and then Gott would gain the advantage over the female singers too. If, even in this case, Kubišová came too high, they would have to destroy the postcards with the votes for her and double the votes for a singer called Eva Pilarová.

The categories were combined and the votes doubled. Gott came first, and Marta was in seventh place.

The Nightingales had always been awarded at a special ceremony, with the top ten winners appearing on television.

The censor gave the following instructions: Kubišová will be awarded her prize at the office, and only the top six performers will take part in the concert.

Copies of *Hot Kittens* were sent to the concert offices, newspapers, radio and television. Neckář describes how they were also sent out to selected individuals—those who were suspected of being enemies of socialism. When the head of a provincial cultural center received an envelope with no sender's name and a picture of the naked Kubišová inside, he immediately felt as if someone were watching him, that they knew something about him, and they were warning him: if you're a naughty boy, we can do something equally horrible to you.

She disappeared.

For twenty years, the radio and television stations didn't broadcast a single song performed by her. She tried to find a job of any kind, but the Security Service made sure she couldn't get one.

She and her husband went to live in a village, in a house left to him by his family. The village was called Slapy.

The word *Slapy* was not allowed to appear in the media.

Journalist Jiří Černý did an interview for *Melodie* magazine with the jazz vocalist Eva Olmerová, who mentioned that she had recently been to stay with friends in Slapy. The editor in chief of *Melodie* personally changed the phrase "in Slapy" to "not far from Štěchovice." "For God's sake," he said, "let's be careful that no one figures it out. Štěchovice is the next little place, and it'll let us sleep in peace."

Marta went to Prague for court hearings—she had sued the head of Pragokoncert for defamation. The court admitted that it was in fact uncertain whether the woman in the pictures was Kubišová. "Perhaps the plaintiff would like to be photographed in identical poses? For comparison and an expert opinion." Her husband reckoned that they were just waiting for pictures like that to have real proof that yes, she did take part in a porno session. She refused. The court ruled that an apology should be made, the head expressed his regret, and the case was closed. Kubišová and her husband realized they had no money left. "A few weeks went by and there was nothing to eat," says Marta.

Her husband, movie director Jan Němec, made inquiries about work in Slapy. They had a job for him as a tractor driver. For her, there would be a job at a food processing plant, chopping up chickens.

As we know, the country didn't immediately change into a Soviet ghetto after the invasion.

Humiliated by the Russians, the party chief Dubček left

his post in spring 1969, and until Gustav Husák replaced him, until his government, imposed by Moscow, had mercilessly suppressed everything it hadn't thought up itself, there was a transitional stage. For a year and a bit, a lot of things were still possible.

After the invasion, Marta still won the Golden Nightingale for 1968. She recorded "Taiga Blues '69" for the radio—a haunting song about the "tender taiga" in honor of eight Moscow University employees who on August 25, 1968 held a protest in Red Square against the invasion of Czechoslovakia. Six of them were sent to labor camps for four years and two were shut up in a psychiatric hospital.

Six months after the invasion by fraternal troops, she put out a solo record. Two months later, the Golden Kids had a premiere at Prague's Rokoko Theater. A year after the invasion, Marta also performed at a song festival in Yugoslavia.

When, towards the end of 1969, the "normalization" began, the émigré poet and singer Karel Kryl described it like this: "Comrades Husák and Bilak have passed a death sentence on Czech culture and made a goulash out of it." The occupying force was no longer needed. "And the Gustapo has smashed us in the face," said Kryl. "Gustapo" was a famous pun he'd made up in honor of Gustav Husák.

The name of a theater in Brno was even changed because of him. *Husák* means *goose*, so instead of *Husa na provázku* ("Goose on a string") it became *Divadlo na provázku* ("Theater on a string").

Marta began to receive anonymous letters: "Miss Kubišová, the songs you sing are shit that demoralizes people."

She used to sing Bob Dylan and Aretha Franklin songs with Czech lyrics.

"The Western leisure industry is influencing revisionist attitudes in Czechoslovakia. An opponent can systematically gradate his ideological sabotage with the help of pop songs. Aided by Western chart toppers, he can cause apolitical attitudes to further demoralize youth, and by the same token create a rabble that would then conduct campaigns against the socialist authorities"—went the analysis of Marta Kubišová's role in Czech society, as published by the East German newspaper, *Neues Deutschland*.

People usually look towards the future to escape from their troubles. They imagine a line across the path of time, beyond which their present worries will cease to exist. Dr. Tomáš's wife Teresa, the heroine of Milan Kundera's *The Unbearable Lightness of Being*, couldn't see any such line ahead of her. The only consolation she had was in looking back.

"I had a bad time," remembers Marta. "Because there was nothing to console me, neither in the future nor the past."

Absolutely nothing.

She became pregnant, but got too upset in court and miscarried in the eighth month; the doctors saved her from a state of clinical death. "Your child was killed by stress," they said when she opened her eyes.

" 'What child? What stress?' I thought. I could only think of one thing: there was some Coca-Cola on the windowsill and I wanted to drink it. Something had wiped my mind clean. Later on, whenever I had to talk about the past, I found a way to avoid it because I couldn't remember anything and whatever I said sounded unreliable. The trauma gradually passed, but even now I have to say everything twice or I don't remember it. Apart from song lyrics."

She used to go back to Prague and walk about the city aimlessly. "When you're walking fast, your thoughts aren't as intrusive," she explains. At the same time, the writer Bohumil Hrabal was travelling up and down Prague in the #17 tram. He'd been interrogated at the Department of Security, and didn't want to be at home, where they might be able to find him again. In the tram, he used to consider ways of departing this world.

Marta roamed Prague with the presentiment: "Something's going to fall on me, a balcony, a cornice, or a flowerpot. A while back, a woman was killed by a falling cornice."

" 'There are lots of old houses in Prague,' I would tell myself. 'The occasional balcony is bound to fall.' But luck passed me by in every way."*

---

* According to Václav Havel, a large cornice fell onto a female passer-by on Vodičkova Street in central Prague in the 1960s. Her death provoked a storm of protest. The authorities channelled the mood by saying in the media that it proved that socialism had made great progress, because the causes of the incident "could be officially criticized."

The atmosphere surrounding the woman's death inspired Havel to write a play called *The Memorandum*, in which the head of a government office receives a memorandum in a weird, complicated language. He is surprised, since his subordinates have learned, sooner than he has, that a new official language called *Ptydepe* is in force. It is meant to improve the organization of work by removing inexact words.

In it, the resemblance between words has been minimized. One of the characters, a Professor Peřin who is a "language activist," explains: "Words must be formed by the least probable combination of letters." There is also a logical principle at work: the more common the meaning, the fewer letters. The word "wombat" has 319 letters, while the Party nomenclature's favourite

• • •

Meanwhile, luck didn't pass Helena by.

She performed at festivals in Split, Bratislava, Istanbul, Knokke and Bucharest. Her crowning achievement was the Grand Prix Sopot '77 for "Malovaný džbánku" ("The Painted Jug"). The song was composed by Jindřich Brabec, who wrote "A Prayer for Marta."

On November 3, 1994, the historian Timothy Garton Ash was sitting in the concert hall at the Lucerna Palace in Prague. He later wrote:

> *Tonight's guest stars are the Golden Kids, a Sixties pop group who haven't performed together for nearly twenty-five years ... When [they] sing "Suzanne" there's just total silence ... Tense and heavy with regret ... There's another story being played out on stage this evening: the story of Marta and Helena ... In the middle of the "Velvet Revolution," Marta Kubišová ... made her first comeback—a moment I will never forget, at once*

---

word, "whatever," consists of just two letters, *gh*. Of course, there is a fallback: a word consisting of the single letter *f*, in case an even more frequently used word than "whatever" should appear.

Ptydepe is meant to be a super-synthetic language, essentially an anti-language. Its users become mechanical beings who have lost the ability to differentiate between actual language and the situation in which it is used.

Why the name *Ptydepe*?

"Why not?" asks Havel. *Ptydepe*, just like the word *kafkárna* (from Kafka: its meanings include an absurdity that is impossible to explain rationally), has settled in the public consciousness for good. Several times—to keep up the conversation—I've asked the drivers of Prague taxis what *Ptydepe* means, and they all knew it was a sort of Newspeak.

rapturous and terribly sad. Barely able to sing, due to
the engulfing emotion, she whispered into the micro-
phone, Časy se mění. "The Times They Are a-Changin'."

He continues:

Helena Vondráčková took a quite different path after
1969. She continued performing and was seen often on
state television. She collaborated. Now their paths have
met again. Will virtue have its reward? Or does none of
that matter anymore?

Helena—tall, blonde, and still very much in practice—
seems to dominate at first. She's younger, more profes-
sional, and the audience knows her from television.
Perhaps they even feel a little easier with her, for most of
them collaborated, too, or at least made little compro-
mises to keep their jobs. Marta—older, shorter, black-
haired—is a shade slower, and you feel the nervousness
in her voice ... People bring bouquets of flowers up on
stage ... and the flower count is going Marta's way ...
a comfortable-looking man in jeans shambles up and
says he'd like to thank all the performers ... "but above
all, Ms. Kubišová." And we all applaud loud and long,
and we know what he's thanking her for, and it's not her
singing this evening—it's for twenty years of silence.

For Helena, 1994 was a wonderful year. Wonderful, because
after all that time she appeared with Marta again. And wonderful too, because she began recording on her own again.

When decommunization began in the Czech Republic, Helena faced a desert. "New, younger people joined the recording labels and radio stations, and they told me: 'Miss Vondráčková, you must bring along a demo tape. We'll listen to your singing, and then perhaps we'll make you an offer.' Out of self-respect I couldn't do that," she says, and falls silent.

For four years, she didn't release a new record.

After a pause, she says: "Did they write about the Polish folk singer Maryla Rodowicz in Poland too, saying she collaborated with the regime?"

She suddenly asks: "What are you most afraid of?"

"I don't know," I say. "Illness, perhaps."

"Because what drives me nuts lately is people who are prepared to do anything for money. I find them really frightening."

For years, Helena's name was linked with that of the communist prime minister Lubomír Štrougal. According to rumor, they had a lengthy affair.

Another rumor said that Štrougal had bought her a sheepskin coat, and that when his wife found out about it, she had knocked out all of Helena's teeth with a champagne bottle. From then on, apparently, she had teeth made of expensive porcelain, paid for—naturally—by Štrougal.

After 1989, she received the first of many anonymous letters addressed to "*Štrougalka* ['Štrougal's woman'] ..."

"I get lots of anonymous letters that dub me *Štrougalka*, *Štrougalova milenka* ['Štrougal's darling'] or *stará Štrougalová* ['old Mrs. Štrougal']," wrote Helena in her last book.

"*Štrougalka*, now it's your turn!" one of them said.

"Were you his *milenka*?" I ask.

"I've never even met the man. I only ever saw him on the TV news. I spent ages wondering where that rumor could have come from, and suddenly I got a letter that shed some light on it. It was from a married couple living in a small place called Příbram, who happened to like me, and were upset whenever someone spoke badly of me. They suggested that I take a close look at Štrougal's daughter, Eva Janoušková. She looked very much like me: she was tall, with a similar way of dressing, she had an identical hairstyle, and even drove exactly the same car in the same color. A green Fiat sports car. She was extremely close to her father, often went to receptions with him, and they used to say goodbye by kissing each other on the cheek in public. Years later I met her, and she greeted me with the words: 'Hello, my alter ego.' That explains the whole mystery."

Ludvík Švábenský, a jazz musician who was Helena's boyfriend for seven years, recalls that whenever he went to a concert or a public reception with her, he felt awful. He didn't know who he really was—boyfriend or bodyguard ... In the eyes of all the Party types, he was a nobody; they looked straight through him like thin air. "They were desperate to shine in Helena's presence, they besieged her almost to the point of indecency, and she would whisper: 'Luděk, help!'"

A later incident occurred in the bar at the Hotel Praha, by which time she was a married woman; everyone knew her husband, Helmut Sickel, and they knew she was very much in love with this German musician, in spite of which the Czechoslovak Communist Party secretary for culture lay across the grand piano, trying to embrace her, panting heavily. The comrade had one single ambition: to talk to Helena.

And she was nothing but nice and kind.

Everybody could see her smiling.

Helena was always smiling.

Marta's father was a cardiologist who was the head of a hospital. She graduated from high school in Poděbrady, and dreamed of studying medicine or philosophy. The school gave her an order, telling her in writing that she had "a duty to become acquainted with the laboring professions." The workplace would transfer her to higher education if she achieved a positive report. It was 1959, and Marta's first job was at a glassworks. To begin with, she ran to the bar to fetch beer for the factory workers, then she picked out glasses and bottles that were below standard. For three years, she kept insisting that she wanted to go to college. "The manager told me that higher education was for the working class, but I wasn't a member of that class," she says, "so I escaped into singing."

She entered music contests and won them. She became a local star, and began singing in a café.

While her father was the senior registrar, they lived at the hospital. When he reached the age of fifty, he went off with another woman. His former family was offered an apartment belonging to the widow of Lieutenant-Colonel Mašín; he had been shot by the Nazis, and his two sons had fled the country before Stalin's death and joined the US army. The authorities had decided to punish his widow by evicting her from her apartment. Before a Party committee, Marta's mother declared that she wasn't going to move in when Mrs. Mašínová left. She found herself an empty apartment opposite the widow's, on the same floor, and made friends with her.

"Yes, Mom had a strong character," admits Marta. "But it was just by chance that I was the one who sang the 'Prayer.' These days, whenever someone tells me I'm some sort of symbol, I run away. After all, any singer could have recorded the 'Prayer.' I'm not politically involved nowadays either. I've just been through a few things. I knew how to tell black from white, and I've always been guided by that."

According to Marta: "Jan wanted to leave. For America. Everything here disappointed him. 'You're good at singing jazz,' he said. But I didn't want to sing in an American bar—I believed I'd soon be back on the stage here, because in two years the Russkies would go home.

"And I waited ten times longer than I thought I would.

"I stayed here. Havel stayed, lots of people did.

"I demanded a divorce.

"The divorce dragged on for ages, I got the feeling I wasn't meant to exist.

"By then, I even felt scared waiting for the tram. I felt as if the driver was going to get out and say: 'Miss Kubišová, you may not get on board. This tram is not for you!'

"Once I was sitting alone at home, and I thought: 'I'll turn on the gas.'

" 'After all, I can't have a child.'

" 'I can't sing.'

" 'I can't even get divorced normally!'

" 'I am a big mistake.'

"And, at that point, a kind of strength kicked in. It came from the animals. I looked at my dogs. 'My God,' I thought. 'What about them?' And I came to my senses.

"When Hrabal used to travel about Prague on the #17 tram, he drew strength from animals, too. I read that it was from swans. Because the seventeen goes along the Vltava."

She found a soothing job. She had a hot iron, a special knife, and a roll of PVC. She cut out a pattern and produced figurines. She assembled little bears out of plastic. There were left and right arms in separate heaps. The legs were all in one pile, because there was no difference between right and left. She had to press them firmly into the bears' bodies, which made her fingers ache badly. "For six years, I either cut or pressed. And the doll-making cooperative that was willing to give me a job was called 'Direction.'"

She worked alone at home, glancing at a small television set. The work was not humiliating.

Jan Procházka's daughter Lenka spent twelve years cleaning a theater. She was forced to give up studying journalism in the radio department. The actors whom Lenka knew from her diction workshops would avoid her in embarrassment when they saw her there with her floor cloth and bucket. And Lenka says she's grateful to them for that. But for Marta, sitting at the kitchen table, nobody had to change their route.

During the normalization, Cardinal Miloslav Vlk spent eight years washing store windows.

The philosopher Jiří Němec was a night watchman for five years.

The writer Karel Pecka worked for six years in the city sewers.

The critic Milan Jungmann spent ten years cleaning windows.

Radio journalist Jiří Dienstbier was a stoker at a boiler house for three years.

Journalist Karel Lánský laid tiles for twenty years.

Historian Jaroslav Valenta, a member of the Academy of Sciences, became a proofreader at a printing house.

For the public statement he made opposing the Soviet occupation, legendary Olympic athlete Emil Zátopek, the track and field star of the late 1940s and early 1950s, was forced to work in a uranium mine.

Journalist Eda Kriseová found herself on a list of authors who couldn't publish, but thanks to friends in high places she became a librarian. She worked alone, so that nobody would be obliged to talk to her. So, in the afternoons, she used to go and talk to the patients at a mental hospital. "There were two nurses caring for seventy patients and they couldn't cope. Nobody ever talked to those people, so I thought: 'They're more desperate than I am, I'll help them.' But it was they who helped me. They opened up the world of storytelling for me. Thanks to those patients, I went on to write two collections of novellas. I realized that, in Czechoslovakia, a hospital for the mentally ill was the only normal place, because there everyone could say what they really thought with impunity."

Just like Eda, Marta has no regrets.

What about regret for all the opportunities that will never come again?

What she was forced to do was no loss. "A person grows

wiser," says Marta. "Not because he's washing windows, but because he's living a life he would never have touched if he were only an artist."

"I've got a child," she adds, "and if I had stuck with singing, I probably never would have had her."

She got married again. To another director, also called Jan. She looked after herself properly. She was careful to avoid stress. She gave birth to a daughter, Katarína. Her husband was happy, and started calling the baby girl Kačenka. "It was Easter Saturday, and our daughter was eighteen months old," says Marta, "when my husband called home to say he wouldn't be back for the night. 'Kačenka has a new little sister,' he said. And so for the past twenty-two years I've been happily divorced."

Maybe Marta is right. Maybe any other female singer of the time might have sung the "Prayer."

However, ten years after the "Prayer," she and the singer Jaroslav Hutka were the only ones who weren't afraid to write a letter to Johnny Cash.

He was due to appear at the Lucerna on the day when the trial of Ivan Jirous was taking place. Known as Magor (meaning "Loony"), the wrongfully arrested Jirous was the inspiration behind the band Plastic People of the Universe. This was the most oppressed, the most outrageous, the most legendary and the most indomitable rock group in the history of Central Europe. What Kubišová and Hutka wanted was for Cash to tell the West about it.

• • •

She was also the only one of the popular stars to sign Charter '77.

The Charter was born on the initiative of Václav Havel, following the trial of the Plastic People musicians.

Legend had it that they performed sexual acts on stage. In fact, they played psychedelic rock. At one of their concerts, they hung up dozens of smoked herrings on strings, dripping oil onto the audience.

In the neo-Stalinist era, lyrics such as: "Sunday morning, what a gas, I really had to scratch my ass" took on special significance.

Nobody had ever treated the audience the way they did.

The hit of the independent music scene was the one-verse "Zácpa" ("Constipation").

The band was formed in Prague in October 1968, two months after the invasion. "Nobody's ever got anywhere …" they sang, and with every performance they infuriated the authorities more and more. They were accused of a lack of respect for the working people, and a series of repressive measures were taken against them.

Special units were even sent to destroy the buildings where they had performed. In Rudolfov near České Budějovice, where they gave a concert in 1974, a motorized militia unit herded a hundred spectators ahead of it like cattle, as the militiamen drove vehicles straight at them. The band and their fans were constantly being charged with hooliganism. A lawyer explained to them that, according to law, hooliganism could only happen in a public place, so, in the 1970s, fans of the Plastics (as they are generally known) began buying up private houses. These were old, ruined country cottages and barns where they could perform. They recorded their best-known album in the barn at Václav Havel's place in the country.

A house not far from Česká Lípa was burned down by the Security Service three weeks after the Plastics had performed there. For two years, the authorities did their best to take official possession of a house in Rychnov, which apart from being a site for concerts, was where the Princ family lived. As soon as they had succeeded, a special unit immediately invaded the farm. "We were still carrying out our belongings," said Mrs. Princová, "and they were drilling holes in the walls for explosive charges. We hadn't even had time to get around the corner before the house was blown sky-high."

However, in their attitude towards the regime, the Plastics instantly became the antithesis of Švejk.

In the underground press, Magor announced that those who produced the official culture were criminals: "To play Bach for tourists from West Germany and not protest against the fact that the Plastics are not allowed to play 'Constipation' is a crime. To stage Shakespeare when there is no right to stage Havel is a crime."

They were tried as parasites.

They defended their right to sing whatever they pleased.

The prosecutor recommended not cutting their hair or letting them shave, and then showing them on television in this unkempt state—as public enemies. On the second day of the trial, Václav Havel left the courtroom feeling upset, and

unable to think about anything else. In Malá Strana, he ran
into a well-known Czech director, who asked where he was
coming from. "From the trial of the underground," he replied.
The director asked if it involved drugs. Havel did his best to
explain the essence of the case to him. The director nodded,
and said: "So what else is new?" "Perhaps I'm being unfair to
him," wrote Havel years later, as president, "but at the time
I was violently overcome by the feeling that people like that
belong to a world I wanted nothing more to do with."

However, he was later to say: "There were various cir-
cles where people immediately understood that the threat
to the Plastics' liberty meant that everybody's liberty was
under threat."

The audience of bold intellectuals who started attend-
ing the Plastics' trials heralded Charter '77. Rejected by the
system, deprived of the opportunity for intellectual development, or even access to libraries, the intellectuals created
an opposition. First, in December 1976 and January 1977, the
Charter was signed by 242 people, and eventually, over the
next few years, by almost 2,000.

The Charter was a manifesto. It came to the defense of
people whom the communists had deprived of their jobs,
forcing them to work in professions that were humiliating
for them.

It was proof of the power of the powerless.

The people who wrote the text called things by their
proper names. "The victims of apartheid" was their term for
the thousands of people who were refused jobs in their own
professions. "Hundreds of thousands of citizens are denied
freedom from fear, because they are forced to live with the

constant threat that, if they express their own views, they will lose their job opportunities."

For all those years, every few days they sent letters, protests and petitions to the authorities within the country and abroad. In 1978, they formed the Committee for the Defense of the Unjustly Persecuted.

The first spokespeople for Charter '77, who represented it to the outside world and guaranteed the truthfulness of the words published as the Charter's texts, were the philosopher Jan Patočka, Václav Havel and Professor Jiří Hájek, Minister of Foreign Affairs during the Prague Spring.

Marta, too, was a spokesperson for Charter '77, and Havel became Kačenka's godfather.

She knew her child was what mattered most. She had to guarantee her daughter a normal life. At the beginning of the 1980s, she returned to Prague from the countryside. "Quite without expecting to, I found a good job," she says. She worked as a report writer at the Prague Urban Development Department. For ten years. Her mother sold a few family heirlooms and her brother sent sums of money from Canada, where he had moved in 1968.

There were usually two cars parked outside the house with people sitting in them. It was easy to tell where the best known opposition activists lived, because each of their homes was watched by two cars. In Prague, there was a story about a Professor Hájek, who used to go running in the park each morning among the trees, where no car could make its way.

Until the Security Service banned the professor from taking physical exercise in the open air.

She always took a toothbrush and toothpaste with her when she went out, in case she had to spend the night at the police station. "They often detained me at around two in the afternoon. Because at three, Kačenka came out of classes and they closed the school. 'Oh! your daughter is just finishing her lessons,' the smug Security Service agent would say. Sometimes they deliberately kept me there until six, and the poor teacher would spend three hours walking around the school with my child."

Marta's eyes are shining.

"Jesus!" she says. "I was always the last mother there. I was half crazy by then. Whenever I couldn't bear it, I'd say to Havel: 'You tell them! Tell them I haven't signed any petitions for ages. And that I want to be left in peace.'"

She drags on her eighteenth cigarette of the day.

"Do you know my song 'Life Is Like a Man'?"

For thirty years, Vondráčková and Neckář have been dogged by the accusation that they kept performing while their friend was "an artist in liquidation."

According to Helena: "People were outraged that we were working. It takes a bit of imagination: I was eighteen years old, Vašek was twenty-three, and Marta was twenty-seven with a husband. At the age of eighteen, I couldn't just sit down on the sidewalk and beg. I was so set on being a singer!"

According to Václav: "They say Helena and I did nothing

for her cause. It's not true. We went to all the official places we could. We even got into President Svoboda's chancellery. His daughter worked there (she was married to the Minister of Culture), and she said that nothing could be done because the cards had been dealt and that was that."

Helena, again: "Should we, throughout the communist era and beyond, have pulled out that sheet of paper and shown it to the audience before every single one of our performances, saying: 'Here is our right to live our lives!'?"

"A sheet of paper?"

"A letter," says Neckář. "Marta wrote us a letter. She was trying to make our lives easier. In black and white."

My Dear Kids, Helenka and Vašek!

Forgive me for writing things that I'd rather be saying to you, but it's better this way, because one day someone might accuse you of not having stood by me. You have behaved fantastically towards me—few people would have shown that side of themselves. Go perform on your own without me. I'm going to be appearing in court, giving explanations, and it'll be impossible for me to perform as if nothing had happened. If you can still work, go ahead and work. Dear Kids, perhaps one day we'll be able to do it all again, but for now we must put off the dream of the 'Invincible Three' for later.

Yours, Marta.
Prague, March 25, 1970.

• • •

To weaken the force of Charter '77, the authorities organized a counter-campaign, known thereafter as the Anti-charter. This document condemned the dissidents, and was designed to scare ordinary people away from wanting any sort of contact with "the enemies of socialism."

Intellectuals, performers and writers from all over the country were summoned to the National Theater in Prague. Each day for a week, *Rudé právo* announced the names of hundreds of people who had signed the declaration of loyalty. Male and female singers were called to the Music Theater on the Friday, so that everybody could read about them on Saturday, February 5, 1977, in the edition with the biggest circulation. The name of a leading translator or architect didn't have the same force as the name of a popular singer.

Karel Gott made a speech.

Gott is the Czech Presley and Pavarotti rolled into one.

He's worshipped in Germany, too. For his single with the German version of the song about Maya the Bee, Karel Gott received five Gold Discs from the recording company Polydor, which represents sales of one and a quarter million copies.

He not only won thirty Golden Nightingales in the socialist era, but went on winning them in the capitalist period too, every year until 2012. He began the 1990s with a triumphal tour which—as the right-wing press spitefully commented—defied reason.

Back then, in 1977, he said that those who had come to the Music Theater "are happier to sing than to speak, yet there are situations where singing is not enough."

He thanked the authorities for providing "the space for

artists to work." The performers signed the declaration: "As Czechoslovak artists, through ever more beautiful music we wish to do all we can to contribute to the march towards a happy life in our homeland."

"In the name of socialism," 76 "National Artists," 360 "Distinguished Artists" and 7,000 ordinary ones signed the Anti-charter.

None of them was allowed to read Charter '77. They were protesting against something they had no idea about.

Nowadays, involvement in the Anti-charter is an attractive topic for the media. They still won't let performers forget about the past for a single moment. Journalist Renáta Kalenská talked to the singer Jiří Korn:

"Did you ever sign a petition?"

"I did."

"Which one?"

"The Charter."

"Seriously? Did you have any problems as a result?"

"No. No problems at all. Quite the opposite. It's just ... When you talk about those petitions, there was one they organized which ..."

"Are you thinking of the Anti-charter?"

"Oh yes—yes, I signed it."

"So you didn't sign the Charter, but the Anti-charter?"

"Yes, the Anti-charter."

"Why was that?"

"Because there was nothing else I could do if I wanted to work."

What accounts for Korn's statement is not just the absent-mindedness of an artist, but perhaps a typically Švejk-like—and thus conscious—form of forgetfulness. Because Švejk's attitude is a prescription for survival. In February 2002, the first weekend edition of the popular Czech daily *Mladá fronta dnes* opened up a debate about why the Czechs can't abide heroes. "Centuries ago, this nation was regarded as a band of armed radicals. Why is Švejk our national symbol now?" asked the editorial, and replied: "Because we know heroism is possible, but only in the movies. And nobody lives in a void."

The newspaper took the opportunity to remind us of the late philosopher (and editor at Radio Free Europe) Josef Jedlička's essays on Czech literary types: "Švejk respects nothing but life itself. And ultimately, whatever makes life more comfortable, pleasanter, and safer." At the heart of this attitude, there is a complete lack of respect for human actions or institutions. This sort of person doesn't give a damn about how he appears before others. "And so for Švejk no price demanded of him for the opportunity to survive will be too great," adds Jedlička.

The thinkers insist: "He is not an accidental clown."

Švejk is the philosopher of cunning acquiescence.

And at the same time, the archetype of adaptation.

"Dear Mr. Husák, why are people behaving the way they do?" Havel asked the First Secretary of the Communist Party Central Committee in 1975. He sent him a letter. He spent two weeks writing it, producing in the end an essay about the moral collapse of society.

In it, he replied to his own question: "They are driven to it by fear."

But not fear in the common sense of the word: "Most of those we see around us are not quaking like aspen leaves: they wear the faces of confident, self-satisfied citizens."

What Havel meant was fear in a deeper sense. Meaning "the more or less conscious participation in the collective awareness of a permanent and ubiquitous danger"; "becoming gradually used to this threat"; "the increasing degree to which, in an ever more skillful and matter-of-fact way, we go in for various kinds of external adaptation as the only effective method of self defense."

In the summer of 1968, when Havel was in the US, he had a meeting there with Czech writer Egon Hostovský, who had emigrated in 1948 immediately after the communist putsch. Hostovský told him that he had emigrated to get away from himself.

He was so terribly afraid of what he might do if he stayed.

After 1989, the editors of *Lidové noviny* posed a question to the performers whose names had appeared on the pages of *Rudé právo* in 1977: "Do you think the fact that you signed the Anti-charter in any way marks you out in public life?"

Musician Petr Janda replied: "No, I don't. I don't think I had to be any kind of a hero."

Slovak comedian and actor Július Satinský: "It doesn't affect me at all. I'm glad there were a lot of us, and we didn't know what it was about."

Oscar-winning movie director Jiří Menzel (who made

Closely Watched Trains): "I don't get that impression. But if Mr. Havel, for example, wanted to judge me, I would feel marked out."* Of course, there's a rhetorical device hidden in that answer. Everybody knows that Havel is far from condemning anyone.

Let's take a look at Gott.

To a similar question, he replies: "But the nation doesn't resent me for having been one of this country's biggest providers of foreign currency. They say I'm like several factories."

He says he was forced to appear at the theater, but he didn't know what it was all about. It was only later when he watched the event on television that he saw how commentary was added, and the whole thing edited and given a new meaning.

"Not once was the term 'Communist Party' uttered there," says Gott in his own defense.

But why did he go? "Of course they didn't hold a knife to my throat," he continues. "But, reading between the lines, I realized that I had to go, otherwise . . ."

". . . otherwise you would never sing again," added the journalist.

"But it's just like today," replied Gott, "if you don't follow the only correct line. In other regimes as well, if you don't

---

* One of the few artists who speaks directly about the disastrous results of being involved in the campaign against Charter '77 is writer and dramatist Karel Hvížďala. His reply to *Lidové noviny*'s question was as follows: "Of course, I disappointed people. At the time I signed the Anti-charter, I wasn't in the Party, despite which various pressures were applied to a person to get him to shake hands with the Devil. I was aware of my own weakness, and I left the country."

keep step with the only correct line, it can end badly, too. We can only guess at the reasons for the deaths of Monroe, Lennon, Morrison and others in the country with the greatest degree of freedom."

The Golden Nightingale knows the inside story. Some time ago, he declared that Israel sponsored Charter '77. There are a lot of things he knows, but he can't make public, because "if I write it all down, I'll be run over by a car."

A month later, he explained in the press that he isn't an anti-Semite. All he meant was that the signatories of Charter '77 were given financial support by the Western powers. "After all, they weren't able to work normally, they could only get jobs in boiler rooms, or cleaning windows. Do you think they'd have survived on what they earned?"

"But a few people from the West came along and helped them," says the woman interviewing him.

"Yes, and I'm very glad of it," concludes Gott.

He has grudges: those who attack him take no notice of the fact that he never sang a single verse in praise of the communist regime. They've just harped on about the Charter, the Anti-charter, Husák, Gott and the Party for the past ten years. "Why is it," he asks, "that the critics, who these days are such heroes, didn't write all that twenty years ago?"

"You would have had to read those things in underground publications, because they wouldn't have made it past the press censorship," notes another journalist.

" 'They wouldn't have, they wouldn't have . . .' " the singer mimics her. "Then why didn't they say it on the radio, on a live broadcast?"

Let's go back to Helena.

She claims she never signed the Anti-charter. She was on tour in Poland at the time. "They added my name without my knowledge."

Helena's case is strange. She was such a big star that—for propaganda reasons—her name (if she herself had added her signature) would have appeared on the front page of *Rudé právo*. Yet she turned up six days after her male and female colleagues, the last one on the list, on an inside page. "They forgot she was out of the country, and when they remembered, they added her name at the last moment. Obviously they'd never print a disclaimer for her," explains one of her colleagues. "We were all young and stupid at the time."

Josef Škvorecký, who co-founded the biggest Czech émigré publishing house in Canada, wrote of his own generation: "But were *we* old and wise then? We too were young and stupid, but with just a tiny bit of bad luck, our stupidity was capable of ruining lives, and not just our own."

A lengthy debate about Helena flared up in the Czech press. (Most of the radio channels play her songs once an hour.)

In letters from readers who defend the star, the same logical argument appears: the general opinion is that the communist daily *Rudé právo* told lies. After all, it didn't tell the truth about the Soviet intervention in 1968, or about life in the normalization period. If we agree that it lied about almost everything, then why wouldn't it have lied about Helena Vondráčková too?

It was Helena herself who put an end to the debate.

She told the press that in those days any sort of protest meant career suicide. "If I had been in the country during the mass signing of the Anti-charter, and if the communists had come to me with it, I would have signed it."

For several years, journalists have tried hard to get to the bottom of what Marta Kubišová really thinks about Helena, Vašek and Karel. What they would find most attractive would be bitter comments.

But Marta keeps quiet and doesn't make judgments.

She says that Gott is a vocal phenomenon.

"And what about the people who crossed the street at the sight of you? Can you ever forgive them?"

"But I don't know whom I would be supposed to forgive. I've always had bad eyesight and I never used to recognize anyone from more than six feet away. Two years ago, I finally had laser surgery, and at last I can see properly. So thank God, I was extremely short-sighted in those days."

About Gott, Marta says he is a man with a flawless soul.

It was he who acted as godfather to Marta Kubišová's new album of Czech blues in 1996.

He popped the champagne and sprayed the first CD with it.

He said that this little disk was just a small payback for the twenty-year debt that could never be repaid.

He was cheered.

Karel is a superb public speaker.

In July 2006, his museum was opened in Jevany, just outside Prague. With a neon sign saying *Gottland* over the entrance.

No living artist—at least in the Czech Republic—has ever had his own museum before, with full-time guides giving tours in three different languages.

Karel Gott is sacred in a desacralized reality.

A world without God is impossible, so in the world's most atheistic country, which is the Czech Republic, the sixty-seven-year-old star plays an important role.

The role of *mein Gott*.

On top of that, in recent years it has been possible to commune with him very closely. Every single book about his love life has been a best-seller: *When the Lovers Weep* (1999); *Marika, or How a Young Girl Found Happiness—Three Years with an Idol* (1999); *In Bed with Gott: A Guide to the Golden Nightingale's Love Life* (2000); *From the Secret Diary of Marika S, or There's Only One Karel Gott* (2001); and *The Composer of Fragrant Lingerie* (2002).

The Gottland museum is in a villa which Gott bought as his summer holiday home. Even though it's a weekday, the parking lot is full of tour buses from all over the country. There's a crowd of old people on the steps. They're upset because only twenty people are admitted at a time, every twenty minutes. Most of the people here are over sixty. Most of them prefer to stay here propping each other up, rather than stepping aside to sit down at the terrace café. There they stand, nervously waving their tickets in their work-ruined hands. It looks to me as if they want to go inside right away. As if here and now, this minute, they want to confirm that their lives have been all right.

They loved Gott, and they made it through communism along with him.

If he "had to keep step with the correct line," then what were we to do?

Getting inside Gottland is like obtaining a seal of approval: the past is okay.

We pass through the "Maestro's" kitchen (that's what the guides call him). "He cooked here often, usually fish dishes," they say. "In the top drawer, you can see the original knives and forks he used when he was already a famous singer."

We all peer into the top drawer.

Let's return to Marta.

At the back of the Church of Our Lady before Týn, near the Old Town Square in Prague, one of the oldest theaters in Europe is run in a basement. It is called Divadlo Ungelt—the Ungelt Theater. Dating back to the fourteenth century, it was a little theater for customs officials, who had their office and accommodation next door. *Ungelt* means "customs duty." The auditorium has thirty seats; it looks like the smallest theater in Europe as well.

Marta Kubišová gives concerts there. Milan Hein, the owner, adores her strong alto voice, which isn't aching to win anyone's favor. Unlike Helena, Marta is reluctant to sing *sladáky*—schmaltzy songs aren't in her style. She kicks off the evening with a blues number, with lyrics by Pavel Vrba:

Life is like a man
Who drives every woman crazy
I trust him, although he's a liar
As twisted as a vine
And yet I believe him
Because he's sent from heaven
Though the heavens can be cloudy
Life is like a man
Who's no stranger to me
He's not a good man
Why do I love him so
When his voice frightens me
He suddenly says "enough"
And he's gone
I'm afraid to see him walk away

At 10 p.m., the small crowd exits the Ungelt Theater into Malá Štupartská Street and collides with a marijuana-scented cloud. Opposite, there's a nightclub. There are drug dealers standing around, or sitting in the road and smiling. Through the club's windows, in the red lamplight you can see the drag queens, lip-synching to playbacks of famous female singers.

In three of the windows, there are three Helena Vondráčkovás.

BETTER PR

It's 2002.

The editors of the weekly *Respekt* have received a letter from a reader who was four years old in 1977.

He thinks that any band that wants to sell well should put some effort into the task. Whenever he goes to a bookstore he can never find anything about Charter '77. The young reader feels that the performers' caution and conspiratorial habits are the reason why "the band Charter '77" has such poor publicity.

"The band Anti-Charter," he claims, "has much better PR."

HAPPY HOLIDAYS!

This is about 1968.

When I'm in the Czech Republic, I like going to second-hand bookstores to look for old annuals and journals.

On one occasion, I found *Dikobraz* ("Porcupine") No. 51, dated December 17, 1968.

Despite four months of Soviet occupation, the country is not yet totally paralyzed by fear. In the satirical weekly, there's a bold festive cartoon: in a few days, it will be Christmas 1968, and two gentlemen are exchanging greetings, saying "Merry Christmas 1989."

Thus, it'll only be a happy holiday in twenty years' time.

How did the cartoonist manage to see the future so precisely?

What did he think of his cartoon when twenty years of despair came to an end at the exact moment he had predicted? In Czechoslovakia, communism really did collapse a month before Christmas 1989. And what did he think three days after Christmas, when Václav Havel was sworn in as president?

Why did that particular year occur to him?

Did he ever make any other prophecies?

Did this drawing have any significance for him afterwards?

I think that anything the cartoonist has to say about this will be worth hearing.

The cartoon is signed "Bape." This turns out to be the pseudonym of Vladimír Pergler, a staff cartoonist at *Dikobraz*. The magazine ceased to exist in 1990, but Bape has his own website, which is maintained by his daughter, Šárka Loty Erbanová-Polcarová. Over the phone, she tells me her dad died in 2001. He was sixty-eight.

His friend Jiří Bartoš, who helped him think up the cartoons ("Bape" is an acronym based on the first letters of their surnames) has also passed away.

I visit the cartoonist's daughter in Prague. On the entrance door into her apartment block there's a nameplate that says NUMEROLOGIST.

She and her mother, Pergler's wife, receive me. They don't actually remember any such cartoon, and are surprised.

"You'll admit," I say, "this is pure prophecy, clairvoyance, or rather clair-drawance!"

"I myself am a numerologist, a fortune-teller, and in fact, I use automatic writing," explains the daughter.

"Automatic writing?"

"Yes, a person in a trance makes contact with a source of energy from outer space and writes. It is a graphic spiritual connection. The medium makes notes, but the words appear on the paper without his conscious involvement. When he comes out of the trance, he is often very surprised by the message passed to him by a higher energy."

"And who can write automatically?"

"Someone who is materialistic, for example, has a lesser chance of conveying messages from outer space."

"It's your dad," I say excitedly. "He must have drawn this message in a trance."

"Or perhaps," puts in his wife, "he just turned the last two digits over? After all, our world was standing on its head in those days, so he put the figures upside-down too. I'm telling you, I'm sure Vláďa didn't know what he was drawing."

THE TRAGEDY HUNTER

Eduard Kirchberger was born in Prague in 1912.

At the same time and in the same place, the world's first Cubist sculpture of a human head was created.

These two facts have no connection.

PART 1: *BRAK*

After the communist takeover in Czechoslovakia, society has to be forced into detox.

The authorities give orders for anything that brings simple pleasure to be liquidated.

Liquidation committees are established. Their task is to remove crime fiction, horror and adventure stories, thrillers, romance novels and science fiction as soon as possible from every outlet. In short, to get rid of every lowbrow form of literature.

The committees scour the bookstores, printing and publishing houses, paying particular attention to secondhand bookstores. There, they requisition countless copies of *Incautious Maidens* or *Flames at the Metropole*. So that those who prefer the false view of the world presented in cheap novels will never find refuge again.

The death of trash is meant to occur in a natural way along with the death of capitalism, in February 1948. But that's not how it happens. So, in 1950, it is announced that publishing even the smallest pocket-sized novel for lunch ladies is an offense against the state.

As the committees can't cope with the book screening, public collection points for trashy books are organized. Elementary school students at the Hloubětín estate in Prague immediately tear the books into very small pieces at the collection point, to make sure they will never go back into circulation. The children enthusiastically rip up *Jasmines Below the Balcony* and *Faces from the Underworld*.

During the campaign, the term "literary *brak*" is used.

Brak, the Czech word for a "lack" or "shortage" of something, can also mean "a piece of trash." Now it is an epithet for something that ruins people's lives. The liquidation records are full of notes saying: "worthless *brak*," "empty *brak*," "mindless *brak*," "American *brak*," "dull-witted *brak*," "sentimental *brak*" and so on. The press explains to the population that *brak* is a bourgeois machine for making profit. Capitalism offers it to the workers to dull their wits.

On the door of the City Library in Prague, there is a sign saying:

> *READERS,*
> *No doubt you appreciate that we no longer lend* brak *(pulp fiction, crime and adventure novels). Do not write out slips for them and do not request them.*

The authorities manage to pulp almost 70 percent of the trashy books in circulation.

"Operation Exclusion, Operation Substitution"—for so it is called—continues in Czechoslovakia until 1958. It's not until the year 2000 that a historian of literature at Charles University, Pavel Janáček, will research and write about it.

The trash is replaced by socialist-realist trash written by new authors.

Three years before, Andy from *The History of a Black Boxer* (1950) would still have declared: "I want you to be my wife."

And Ruth would have replied, her voice softening: "Darling, you have no idea how much I love you."

Now their romantic exchange can't serve their personal aims alone. So Ruth adds: "We must get to grips with life, like all working people. But you will never be victorious alone. You are a part of the community."

In another book, written in 2003, Pavel Janáček and his colleague Michal Jareš also investigated the biographies of more than a hundred pre-war authors of cheap fiction.

Almost all of them fail to reappear under the new system.

Many writers try their best to forget about their own pasts. "As soon as my books were removed from the libraries as worthless *brak*, I immediately gave up writing, and now I'm trying to erase my literary sins from memory," the author of *Hungry Heart,* Marie Kyzlinková, explains to the Literary Institute in the 1960s. Once she has wiped out her sins, she occupies herself exclusively—as the wife of a railroad inspector—with housework.

Many authors are eliminated forever. The communists

refuse to accept their pledges to become better writers. Jova Patočková assures the Ministry of Information in writing: "In my novel *The Spellbound Seeks a Shadow,* a girl of impeccable character triumphs. As a socialist, I know what normal life is like. In my book, I contrast a girl with a positive attitude to work with a woman from the past who is idle, wanton, and flirtatious."

The Ministry doesn't believe Patočková and refuses its consent to publish the novel; the author is excluded from public life.

There is just one author who manages not only to eliminate himself, but also create his own substitute.

To begin with, he is called Eduard Kirchberger.

Afterwards, he is Karel Fabián.

He is two completely different authors.

The successful metamorphosis takes him three years. The socialist-realist literary reference books do not mention Fabián's past.

In his new incarnation, he even signs his name with different handwriting.

Kirchberger writes about ghosts, monsters, wizards, gunslingers and murderers. Fabián writes about workers, partisans, communists and enemies of the people.

The former writes about terrifying open graves, with women lying in them whose hearts have been ripped out after death. The latter writes about terrifying exploiters who get rich at the expense of the workers.

The former plays up phantoms. The second plays up production achievements.

The former adores mysterious caves, dungeons, rock temples and cellars full of demons. The latter—if he ever writes about a cellar—will make it the headquarters of agents of American imperialism.

"I was very surprised," says Pavel Janáček, "when I realized that these two stylistically disparate writers were one and the same person. His adaptation to communism was impressive."

"He was a born storyteller," he adds. "He thought up stories as easily as other people breathe. If he had lived in the US, a single one of his horror stories would have bought him an expensive car. So he couldn't possibly keep quiet just because the communists had come to power. And that's the reason why he brought Kirchberger's life to an end."

PART 2: THE REASON

Did he find the metamorphosis painful?

Is a person who does all he can to win the favor of the totalitarian authorities at the same time trying to endear himself to everybody else?

Does he like being a toady?

Is there any situation where he is capable of saying "No"?

Did his new self become more important to him than the old one?

Karel Fabián is asked what he did before the war. In the official biographies, he mentions "publications." "I don't rate them at all," he immediately adds, although Kirchberger's tales enjoyed success.

The system must be aware of his transformation. So why

do the communists treat his metamorphosis with such understanding, while excluding a hundred other authors from
public life?

"That's the most curious part. Maybe you'll look into it?"
Pavel Janáček encourages me.

Eduard Kirchberger / Karel Fabián died in 1983, and since
then twenty-two years have gone by. I start by looking for
people who knew him and scouring the archives.

I find one daughter in Germany. She used to be a journalist in Bratislava, but she emigrated in 1980. She and her
husband and son pretended they were going on holiday to
Sweden. "We were on our guard throughout the journey," she
says, "to make sure we only talked about trivial things in the
car. So the regime wouldn't realize anything was up, if they'd
put a bug in there."

It all began to come apart for her when she witnessed
an aerial disaster—a plane full of people had crashed into a
reservoir near Bratislava. The aircraft was stuck nose down,
and the passengers sitting at the back had suffocated. Nobody
knew how to get them out of there. There was a crowd of
people standing on the shore, and the militiamen ripped the
film out of their cameras. When she got back to the newspaper office, her boss asked her why the hell she had gone there,
and if anyone had checked her ID. She said she wanted to
write about it. "Forget it," she heard. "And just remember—
airplanes never crash in our country."

"When he heard I'd fled abroad," the journalist daughter
tells me, "our dad was dumbstruck. He'd spent years whacking

me over the head with his communist views. It's a good thing he was already retired by then and wasn't writing, or he'd have had a lot of trouble because of me."

I find a second daughter, a retired secretary, in Prague. She didn't leave the country. She has just been watching a rented horror movie. Her grandson brings them, and they try to tot up one movie per day.

For years on end, she lived with her mother. Unfortunately, Fabián's wife died a month ago. "And before that she burned all his notebooks. In fact, I'm curious about his life myself. Did he change himself into Fabián to survive?"

Under the new regime, K.F. employs his talents in this manner: "Our manufacturing plants," he writes, "are the stomach of the state. Coal is its heart. Electricity, steam, and gas are its blood."

It is 1949, and the Five-Year Plan starts up. It is assumed that, thanks to the plan, everyone will be well dressed and well fed, life will be beautiful, and nobody will have any existential problems. K.F. becomes a reporter for the weekly *Květen* (meaning May) in Prague. He makes his debut on the back page, but soon almost every edition opens with one of his reports. An article of his titled "The Five-Year Plan Versus the Centuries" wins the heart of the editor in chief.

"What is an electric floor polisher, an electric washing machine, an electric cushion, or an electric baby bottle?" he asks in one of his pieces.

And gives the reply himself: "They are servants of the Five-Year Plan."

In "Problems with Bricks," he stresses that nowadays the foundation of the family is not children, but bricks. "Bricks are bread. Bricks are a house. Bricks are heaven on earth."

By the third month of the plan, in his report from a textiles plant, the personnel clerk, delighted by the new order, states: "We live a fairy-tale existence . . . And everyone is good. There are no bad or insincere people among us."

K.F. should be the happiest writer of 1949—because he publishes Czechoslovakia's first socialist-realist novel.

It's called *About the Power Station*, and it is published on the first anniversary of the victory of communism in Czechoslovakia.

Except that two days before that victory, E.K. was still an anti-communist.

Before the war, he published in *Národní listy* ("National Letters")—the organ of the National Democratic Party—which, before Czechoslovakia came into being, was the monarchy's leading journal for the Czech bourgeoisie. In 1937, after the death of philosopher and president Tomáš Garrigue Masaryk, the founding father of Czechoslovakia, whom the communists would systematically denigrate, he published a poem in which he promises to shed blood and give up his life for Masaryk and for democracy.

After the war, E.K. turns up in Liberec.

He smiles without opening his mouth.

He works at a bank, and publishes his stories in a social-democrat weekly, *Stráž severu* ("Northern Guard"). For three years following the war, Czechoslovakia is the last democratic state in the Soviet bloc. The communists only have 40 percent of the seats in parliament, the national socialists are in second place, and then come the peasant parties and the social democrats. The editor in chief at *Stráž severu* is a democratic member of parliament called Dr. Josef Veverka.

On February 20, 1948, when twelve non-communist ministers resign from the coalition government they have formed with the communists—and by doing so initiate the complete takeover of power by the Communist Party of Czechoslovakia in the course of the next five days, later known as "Victorious February"—E.K. writes a letter to his editor:

Dear Pepíček,

I'm writing to wish you even greater strength. From what I've heard about events in Prague, I guess that any moment now they'll be coming to lock you up. Now I can see the weaklings around me, who are only turning to the left because, as they say, they 'have a family,' but luckily those people are not in our ranks.

So I'm writing to you, Pepíček, to say that you can fully count on me, just as you can on all of us whom you have raised here in Liberec. We are ready to go to jail, because we know that communism is totalitarianism, and we have fought against totalitarianism in every form. Perhaps communism will last as much as a year, but freedom will come, for such are the laws of nature.

You can believe these words, which suddenly came pouring out in my little office, of their own accord.

Early that morning, he leaves the letter on Veverka's desk,

but the editor will never read it. An hour later, the communist who hands the envelope to the Security Service becomes editor in chief of *Stráž severu*.

The letter ends with the words: "So we're going to roll up our sleeves and go against the grain. My two daughters' freedom is worth the effort. Yours, E.K."

Except that, not long after this letter, E.K. begs the Communist Party of Czechoslovakia (the CPC) to accept him as a member.

He assures it: "It was only following the Victorious February that I gave communism proper thought for the first time. To me, communism is like the gospel."

He stresses: "Please note that I want nothing from the CPC, and I never shall. I can say of myself that no part is being played by any motive of fear or calculation, which has brought so many people to the Communist Party. I have come to my own conclusions independently. I do not know how you will judge my case, but if you do not accept me, you will be spurning a man of good will."

He makes excuses for the other letter: "I was told about Veverka, and I felt great sympathy for him. On the night I wrote that fatal letter I had worked on *The Tragedy Hunters* until almost dawn, and once I had finished, after drinking an ocean of black coffee, I couldn't get to sleep. Unfortunately, I ended up in a miserable mood, full of hazy sympathy, and I had to find an object for my feelings. By an unhappy coincidence, I remembered Veverka. It occurred to me that he had a family, that he probably wanted to be a government minister, and so on. I sat down at my typewriter and wrote that letter, then immediately forgot what was in it. I realize it seems hard to believe, but all manner of things can happen to a writer at night."

He gives the Party some advice: "Communism should be taught from the pulpit, with a Bible in hand—not in the church sense of the word of course, but by going among the people and teaching them."

He makes a confession: "I should be sincere enough to admit that I have to study an idea for several years before I can work for it successfully."

(*The Tragedy Hunters* never appeared—most likely he never wrote a single line of it.)

E.K. becomes part of a wider trend.

Václav Kopecký, one of the chief ideologues of the CPC, is surprised to find that non-communist members of parliament are voting unanimously for communist decrees, and even for the non-democratic constitution of May 9, 1948. "It was quite unpleasant," he will write years later, "because this sort of unanimity looked like compulsion. The communists even asked some of the MPs to vote against, or at least to abstain, and gave them guarantees that nothing would happen to them—but in vain. They unanimously voted in favor."

At the end of his request to join the Party, E.K. adds that he is not from a bourgeois family, his father was a servant, and then a clerk, and his grandfather was a tailor.

Except that just after his burst of passion for communism, E.K. flees the socialist country.

The communists aren't hiding the fact that they will crack down on whomever necessary. The Security Service immediately puts the ministers who have resigned under surveillance. The former Minister of Justice (a democrat called Prokop Drtina) tries to kill himself. The Minister of Foreign Affairs (Jan Masaryk, son of the former president) is found on the flagstones under his window with a broken skull. Some people think he jumped because he disagreed with the new system. Others believe it was the new system that had him thrown out of that third-floor window.*

---

* The debate about whether Jan Masaryk jumped from the window or was pushed out of it is now in its seventh decade. Viktor Fischl, a Czech writer who emigrated to Israel and was the former Israeli ambassador to Poland, was Masaryk's secretary during the war. A few days before his death in May 2006, he gave an interview to the weekly *Reflex* in which he went back to this matter. He said that Jan Masaryk was a deeply religious man. "And so is it impossible for him to have jumped out of the window?" asked the journalist. "He can't have done it," said Fischl. "I was never in any doubt. But on the other hand, I saw how his Western friends were unable to understand him, they couldn't see why he joined the communist government. I saw how he was unable to explain it to them, how he suffered as a result, and that torment took him nowhere. At the time I thought to myself, that man is so unhappy he could do anything. Afterwards, however, other things came to light. Dr. Karel Steinbach wrote that Masaryk kept sleeping pills on his bedside table, and Steinbach himself told him: 'Honza, you can take one or two tablets. If you took a third, you certainly wouldn't have time for a fourth.' In 1990, I was a member of the Israeli delegation that made diplomatic contact with Czechoslovakia. Dienstbier was still the minister at the time. He invited us to dinner at the Černín Palace [seat of the Czechoslovak, and now the Czech Ministry of Foreign Affairs]. I was sitting next to him, when suddenly he asked if I would like to see Masaryk's apartment. He took me upstairs. I knew that apartment, because I had often been to see Jan. He showed me the bathroom, too. Jan Masaryk was a big guy, he must have weighed over 220 pounds. It was physically impossible for him to get to the window from which he was supposed to have jumped. He would have had to climb up there on a ladder. I tried to imagine that giant climbing up to the window with difficulty, in order to jump out of it, while, beside the bed, he had sleeping pills which he only had to swallow for all his problems to cease to exist, and I said to myself: it's out of the question."

Nobody can leave the country anymore.

When a certain comedian performs for the soldiers guarding the border, he and his family manage to escape to West Germany during the interval. At that particular moment there's nobody on guard, because they're all waiting for the second half of the show to begin. The leader of the national socialist youth movement escapes by sliding between the ceiling and roof of the restaurant car of a train going from Prague to Paris. The leader of the social democrats and his wife put on skiing outfits and get across to Austria by pretending to be skiers. The former ambassador to Bulgaria escapes by hiding in a large chest for books, which the Mexican ambassador claims as his personal luggage.

E.K. has still had no reply from the CPC. Someone at the bank tells him he might be arrested for the letter to Veverka, because it was critical of the Czechoslovak people. So, at all the kiosks in Liberec and Prague, he starts to buy up the ignition stones that are in cigarette lighters. He knows they can be used as a currency in Germany. He hides the stones with a friend who is a customs officer, whom he urges to flee the country as well. E.K. confides in him that if he doesn't escape, he'll commit suicide. He weeps.

They escape on the day E.K. comes home from the bank and sees a militia car outside his house.

In Berlin, he tells his interrogators that his country is in the grip of the red terror, and that no honest person can possibly live in that communist hell.

Except that two months later he goes back.

In the press, he publishes a cautionary novel in installments. He signs it with the pseudonym František Navrátil, which in Czech means "he came back."

The story can be summarized as follows. One night, Navrátil and a friend swim across the Nysa River near Hrádek, on the German border, aiming to get away to London. They wade through swamps and spend hours lying in a field. Navrátil falls ill with a temperature of 39 degrees C [102°F], but nobody will give him a sip of water until he shows his documents. "Maybe because I have nothing to pay with. People in the West have to be bought."

For those who read it, it should immediately be clear why Navrátil came back. There is no refugee camp in Germany which our heroes have not visited. Nowhere do they find help or a crust of bread. "We only help people who are useful to us," they hear. "When you talk to them about ideals," he confides in his readers, "they start to smile pitifully. They have no ideals—instead of using their brains to think, they use the contents of their pockets."

Fainting with hunger, they reach Hamburg on foot. In the suburbs, they look into a window and see a married couple quarrelling. "How can they be quarrelling when they have their own table, their own floor, their own ceiling, and their own language? What fools people are."

The authorities are so pleased by this account, which appears in the weekly *Květen*, that Navrátil also broadcasts it as radio talks. Then he describes his escape in a novel entitled *The Runaway*, which is publicized by the authorities.

"I think he had to write it," says his daughter nowadays. "He came back to us, because Mom couldn't manage, but he was extremely scared of being punished. That book was his way of buying himself out of the ordeal that might have befallen him."

Except that the regime announces an amnesty for runaways, who are no longer under any threat (something his daughter can't have known about, as she was a little girl at the time). E.K. takes advantage of this.

Even children run away from Czechoslovakia. For example, in the month after the Victorious February, the secret police in Budějovice alone catch eight boys on the border. The European press publicizes these escapes, and the authorities have to make a grand gesture. Thus, E.K.'s future ordeal is canceled.

Except that, despite the amnesty, E.K. wants to show extra gratitude for being treated so leniently. He offers to cooperate with the Security Service.

But before this happens, he tells a friend about his escape, and the friend informs the Ministry of Internal Affairs, which summons the writer to meet with Major Bedřich Pokorný in Prague. The Voice of America describes the Major as "the republic's red executioner," and the executioner himself describes his own investigative methods as "pins and screwdrivers." The Major is acquainted with the great lyric poet Halas and is capable of lecturing on French painting and its influence on Czech art.

Pokorný calls ten journalists in to the Ministry, who are to listen to E.K. They are impressed by his story.

"At that point I realized my political mistake," as K.F. will later confess. "Solely because the people's organs and Major Pokorný treated me very decently after my return."

It is Pokorný, deputy head of the Department for Special Operations, who suggests that he write (as Navrátil) about his escape and his return.

He also suggests that he write a separate book about him, the Security Service major, and the screenplay for a movie. The Major already has a title for it: *I Came to Shoot*.

E.K. sees him as his protector. "In the evenings," he will later say, "he often sent a car for me, and we would discuss Marxism, a topic in which the Major was an excellent teacher for me."

(Not long after this, the Security Service will arrest its own major. For using Gestapo methods during interrogations and for tolerating former Gestapo collaborators among the secret police officers. The penalty: sixteen years in jail.)

In the meantime, Pokorný allows E.K. and his family to move to Prague and gets him a job at *Květen*. That is where E.K.—now as K.F.—writes about the Five-Year Plan.

At this point, despite already having committed to writing the book about Pokorný, he spontaneously suggests that he can also recruit informers working for several other journals.

Except that he immediately tells everybody in his circle that he is an agent and is trying to form a network.

(When he is later arrested for this—betrayal of a state secret—he will insist on a single explanation: "I said it because I wanted to feel that I was a better person than those to whom I was saying it.")

Except that there is one thing he never talks about at all: a month after returning from Germany, he informs on a woman, whose life he destroys in the process.

She is Žofia V., a rich widow, owner of a tenement house on the Vltava River next to the National Theater, where she used to receive senior SS officers. As there are rumors going around about K.F., implying that he is a Western agent, the woman seeks him out and asks him to help her escape. She would like to get as far away from Czechoslovakia as possible in a month's time. She thinks that she'll be smarter than Ida L.—recently featured in the press—who was arrested with well over six pounds of twenty-dollar gold coins glued to her chest with sticking plasters.

K.F. promises to help her, and goes to reveal all to the Major.

Pokorný virtually jumps for joy at the fact that his good deed towards K.F. has paid off; this is a big case that will earn him praise, and next morning they'll be locking up Žofia V.

Except that in the evening K.F. goes to warn her.

They meet in a café. "I had pangs of conscience," he will later admit, "and I advised her to get away immediately, not in a month's time. She said she hadn't amassed enough jewelry yet, and left. As if she hadn't absorbed the fact that next day they were going to imprison her."

She is arrested at dawn. A week later in jail, she swallows poison and dies.

Eduard Kirchberger was born in Prague in 1912.

At the same time and in the same place, the world's first Cubist sculpture of a human head was created.*

These two facts have no connection.

Nonetheless, E.K./K.F. is a Cubist personality. If, in a Cubist picture, the planes are fragmented by countless sharp edges, then, in his life, the successive "except thats" are the sharp edges.

Everything that for the moment seems certain instantly changes direction. His personality—like an object or a figure in Cubism—is in a state of repeated fragmentation.

Maybe it wouldn't have been, if not for fear.

PART 3: PLAYBACK

Fear is highly relevant.

Early in 1951, some Prague intellectuals, who are enemies of the system and have been removed from their professions as a punishment, are building a railroad bridge across the Vltava, which to this day is known as the Bridge of the Intelligentsia.

The CPC now starts to lock up Party comrades, even before they have committed any misdemeanors. Major Pokorný says that it's not only dead traitors who are suspicious. "If

---

* The sculptor was Otto Gutfreund.

someone is alive, he's always a suspect, because foreign agents can contact him," he explains to his subordinates.

They put the writer Lenka Reinerová in solitary confinement for fifteen months, not even letting her out into the prison yard; whenever she asks what she has been arrested for, she invariably hears: "You know better than anyone." Finally, they release her without a trial, and drive her to a park on the edge of town. When she gets home, she discovers that her husband and daughter have been evicted, but nobody knows where they've gone, and somebody else is living in her apartment. She finds them living in a shack sixty miles from Prague. (Several years later, when she wants a certificate to prove that she was arrested, it will turn out that no case like hers ever existed. "Maybe you just imagined it all, comrade," the Ministry of Internal Affairs will tell her.)

The Party takes vengeance on its own members.

The country is gripped by the trial of eleven senior officers, called the Slánský group, who are accused of forming a conspiracy. The wife of one of the defendants sends an open letter to the CPC, in which she asks the court to punish her husband just as he deserves. In a letter to a newspaper, the son of another defendant firmly demands the death sentence for his father. And one of the accused asks for the court to hang him as soon as possible, for "the only good deed I can still perform is to provide a warning for others."

Only a short time ago, agent 62C/A saw K.F. like this: "He is honorable and patriotic. His weak side, however, is uncritical gratitude."

K.F. suddenly stops being a journalist for *Květen* and is not entitled to write about the Five-Year Plan.

He is thrown out.

The CPC Central Committee's Press Department realizes there's something not quite right about him. He muddles up the terms *úderník* ("shock worker"), *předák* ("foreman") and *stachanovec* ("Stakhanovite"), using these concepts as it suits him. He is slavishly loyal to an optimistic vision of the Plan. He miscalculates the percentages by which factories exceed the Plan. Sometimes he overstates them.

In his final report for *Květen*, he takes the liberty of writing: "Shunter Jaroslav Šmíd increased productivity by 33 percent. We could report figure after figure like this, except that figures are lifeless. The things that are alive are people and labor. Whatever we write today, especially figures, may be different tomorrow."

Both he and the editor in chief (the man who was so thrilled by "The Five-Year Plan Versus the Centuries") are both fired towards the end of 1949, and a series of unpleasant interrogations lies ahead of them.

What were they thinking?

Why are figures "lifeless"?

Why aren't they "just as important as people and labor"?

On whose instruction could such a sentence have appeared?

Why exactly is this shunter's productivity being disparaged?

Is the point of it to ridicule the worker Šmíd?

Or maybe to make fun of the entire working class?

Now it is K.F. who is to become a laborer. He will work at an automobile factory. Later, at a factory making decorative products, he is promoted to manager of the textiles department. ("Nevertheless," he will say years later, "I went on writing books with socialist content for my own pleasure.")

He is arrested just as the Slánsky affair is erupting. In the spring of 1952, he is sentenced to six years for betrayal of the state, in other words for broadcasting the fact that he has been cooperating with the Security Service. He comes out after two years, because some sentences are revised after Stalin's death. He becomes a worker again, and until the early 1960s, he casts metal at the Stalingrad II Foundry.

His talent refuses to leave him in peace.

He writes about a dozen popular novels, including *The Riddle of the Five Cottages*—about a group of boys who accidentally discover a nest of spies; *Canine Commando*—about a prisoner in a Nazi camp who looks after dogs that are trained to kill, and whose life is saved by his favorite dog when he escapes from the camp; and *The Flying Horse*—about the war in South Korea.

He comes back into favor and becomes a television screenwriter.

He still laughs without opening his mouth.

He still isn't a member of the CPC.

Not in the least discouraged, for adults he writes fine things about the Security Service.

For children, he publishes fantasy stories in the weeklies.

He never says a bad word about anybody—that's how he is remembered. He is nice to everyone. He has rosy cheeks, a red nose and ears that stick out. He takes his daughters to the bar. He knows how to find his place in society. "Compare her with any cathedral you like, and a woman is always young," he declares to the delighted company. As he is approaching seventy, his friends ask: "Karel, why don't the characters in your books ever screw?" He replies: "I never get to do it, so I'm not going to let them either."

"Don't send my fee to my home address," he asks at the editorial offices, "or Madame will see it." (Everyone calls his wife Madame.) This way he loses out, because getting paid might have been the one occasion when she'd cuddle up to him.

His daughters think he's longing for love.

A close friend thinks that he has never stopped being an only child, who wants to please everyone all the time, without ever losing either his mom's or his dad's affection.

His professional colleagues think he avoids altercations and arguments. They also notice that at official ceremonies he both does and doesn't sing the "Internationale." Everyone else sings out loud, but he just moves his lips.

As one of his colleagues says: "With Karel, it's always the playback."

But on one matter, he is principled.

He will not tolerate lies from his daughters.

For telling lies, he's capable of slapping them across the face. "If you admit it," he says, "I'll let you off!"

Once she is an adult and has managed to get away, the daughter in Germany writes him a letter: "The problem we had in common, Dad, was that you demanded almost boundless obedience from me, but you never explained to me why exactly I had to be obedient."

He succeeds in joining the Party in August 1968, twenty years after the first attempt. "It was the time when only decent people joined," stresses the daughter from Prague.

The only decent moment in the history of the CPC had just gone by—the Prague Spring.

Despite being a sort of miracle, it kills Major Pokorný.

The former security agent has been at liberty for years. He can't accept a state of affairs where open debate, allowing for a contrary opinion, is no longer treated as an affront against the state. He writes a farewell letter: "A communist from the Victorious February of 1948 cannot survive such a terrible defeat for the CPC. This defeat has deprived me of spiritual and physical equilibrium," and places the noose around his neck.

The illusion that the communists themselves are capable of democratizing the regime only lasts for a few months— until the Soviet Army tanks and those of four of its allies roll in. While under the leadership of First Secretary Dubček, the Party continues to be morally opposed to its Soviet brothers. And a week after the invasion, K.F. declares in the newspaper *Svoboda* (meaning "Freedom," and still free for the moment) that he is joining the CPC: "These days, it is a very simple matter, no great words are needed," he starts his letter. "If only because yesterday," he adds, "before my very eyes, our brothers killed a fourteen-year-old boy. And also because the situation is violent, and no one joining the CPC can expect any advantage. He's more likely to get a bullet. I think it's a form of betrayal to stand aside during the fighting. Karel Fabián, writer."

The newspapers print other letters from people who, in

protest against the invasion, have also decided to support the Czechoslovak communists against the Soviet ones by joining the Party.

Except that some of them immediately resign from it.

The terror committed by the Security Service and the normalization as instituted by Husák deprive them of any illusions.

Once Czechoslovakia is back in the Stalin era, K.F., not in the least bit alienated, goes on writing fine phrases about the Security Service in the weekly *Květy* ("Flowers").

As part of their ruthless destruction of the founders of Charter '77, the authorities supply the editors of *Květy* with intimate photos of Ludvík Vaculík, one of the Charter leaders, for publication. Removed from a secret drawer in his desk by security agents, they show him naked, with his lover, in the outhouse at his allotment. His wife finds out about the pictures and the lover from the newspaper. "We wonder why the Western journalists lap up every word that falls from his lips," says the editorial commentary.

K.F. provides *Květy* with a story about a boy who encourages a young salesgirl to steal money from the store, and then leave for the West. He smothers her with a pillow before they manage to go abroad. The Security Service has no trouble finding the murderer in only a week. The city breathes a sigh of relief.

The author takes the opportunity to write: " 'Keep quiet,' the boy's adoptive father often told him. And once added: 'There are people who agree with everything in silence. And now, as an older friend, I'm advising you to do just that.' 'The flagpole is what matters,' he went on. 'After all, a flag of any color at all can fly from it.' "

The secret of why he smiles without ever opening his mouth isn't widely known in K.F.'s circle.

And out of tact, nobody ever asks why he does it.

Always chatty, he never mentions the fact that it was the Gestapo who knocked out all his teeth.

Nor does he say that, from February 1942 until May 1945, he was a prisoner in the Nazis' Straubing fortress.

Or that he underwent ninety-four interrogations, forty-two of which were severe.

Or that he was subjected to six weeks' solitary confinement, in total silence. In winter, the temperature in the cell was only 2 degrees C [35° F].

Or that, on another occasion, he was forced to go two weeks without food.

Or that, when he was not being punished and was allowed to eat, the daily ration was three ounces of bread and nothing more.

Or that he was part of the Nazi "extermination through labor" operation.

Or that whenever there was an air raid, all the prisoners were deliberately herded to the top floor, where they were locked in a single cell in groups of at least thirty. That was when many of them succumbed to insanity.

Or that whenever a prisoner died, the corpse was left among the living for a long time on purpose.

Or that he returned to Prague with a leg injury and broken elbow joints.

He never mentions any of this at all.

This is strange, because old soldiers generally share their experiences. K.F. has a fine record—during the occupation, he belonged to an underground organization. At the Slavia Insurance Association in Prague, where he worked after dropping out of his legal studies, he distributed the biggest underground journal, *V boj* (meaning "Into Battle"). It wrote about national traitors and published patriotic poems.

In just two months, the Gestapo arrested about a hundred distributors. He was tried in Berlin, and imprisoned in Straubing. The sentence: eight months incarceration for making preparations to betray the state.

"Don't mention it in public and don't urge me to talk about it," he asks a colleague at *Květy*. "I don't want to make a heroic act out of it."

The colleague says: "Karel was no martyr."

Except that:

"In 1942, when I was arrested by the Gestapo, in the course of excruciating interrogation, I betrayed all thirteen members of an organization to whom I had delivered the journal *V boj*. They were all imprisoned, and two of them were tortured.

"Through my betrayal, I brought misfortune to fourteen families, because I also betrayed my first wife and her parents.

"When I came back from Straubing to my former workplace, I wrote a letter begging for my crime to be forgiven.

"I received a request from those mentioned above asking

me to leave Prague if I didn't want trouble. They did not wish to encounter me.

"I decided to withdraw, and left for Liberec, where I was employed in a bank as a secretary. Then I started writing for *Stráž severu.*"

He tells this story at one of his interrogations after the war.

We don't know if the Security Service used this information against him.

Towards the end of the 1940s, even the most popular writers are no longer celebrities. Their pictures don't appear in the press. If this confession is to be believed, enticed by Pokorný's offer of the opportunity to live and publish in Prague, E.K. returns from Liberec and invents a new name for himself, so that the old one won't be noticed and cause offence. And most probably, that protects him from being recognized.

For "Operation Exclusion, Operation Substitution," this is good timing.

In 1961, when he returns to favor following his period of enforced labor, his novel *The Flying Horse* is published. It's about the war in South Korea. An American officer travels there to see the results of the mass murder in which he took part. He goes to a village where women and children were killed because of him, and he is recognized. Suddenly, he develops a high fever. The locals tell him they have no wish to see him, but as he is sick, they won't refuse him aid. They will leave food at his door, and then smash every dish he has touched.

In his delirium, the officer reaches the conclusion that he should write a book in which there will only be one truth: if a man kills, he shouldn't go on living. All he can do is exist, because he finds the thought that every dish he touches must be smashed unbearable.

One would have to re-read the vast number of stories which Fabián wrote after the war to find out whether or not he burdens all his negative characters with his own sense of guilt.

In both phases of his life, he has to write a capital letter K whenever he signs his name.

According to a graphologist, the first man's letter K is large, simple and sincere.

The second man's K is also large, but it is propped up.

In various different versions, it has extra feet, flourishes and props. As if it were incapable of holding itself up unaided.

KAFKÁRNA

It's 1985.

Joy Buchanan arrives in Prague, a student on a scholarship who wants to discover Kafka's world. She is writing a paper on him. She can speak Czech, so she walks about the Old Town asking one single question: "Have you ever read Kafka?"

People don't answer. It is 1985, and right away they want to know if she has written permission.

"For what?"

"A document proving you have the right to ask that sort of question."

Miss Buchanan (as she will be called at Charles University) starts going round with a Czech female interpreter and a tape-recorder. This is supposed to increase her credibility. No one has read Kafka, but the passers-by often smile enigmatically and say: "Oh yes, *kafkárna*!" But the interpreter never translates that word.

Finally, the student asks her: "What does *kafkárna* mean?"

"Oh, it's nonsense," says the interpreter and stops talking. But Joy Buchanan refuses to leave it at that. "Well, that word simply shouldn't be used, or rather it can't be used," explains the interpreter at last.

"You have words that can't be used?"

"No, we don't have any forbidden words, of course not. It's just that that word doesn't appear anywhere."

"But people keep saying it!"

"Yet if you were to look for it in writing, you wouldn't find it. And in our country anything that isn't written doesn't really exist. And I'll tell you frankly, that suits everyone fine."

A café is a place where coffee is made, thinks the American, a *vodárna* in Czech is a place where water—*voda*—is purified, and an *octárna* is where vinegar—*ocet*—is made. So there must be a place where something is done with Kafka.

Joy Buchanan starts asking on her own initiative. Her advisor at the university says the word *kafkárna* describes something everyone knows about, but which they also know nothing can be done about. And there's no reason to be surprised. Instead, one should just accept it.

"But accept what?"

"It's something subconscious in people's minds. If you're going to live here for a while, you're sure to get your head round it and suddenly you'll say: 'Aha, *kafkárna*!' "

The people on the Old Town Square give various answers. "It's a joke, and if you didn't take it as a joke you really wouldn't understand it." Or: "It's something very silly, but that has to be." "You must be confusing it with *švejkárna*, but that's bad too, because there's no such word. But there is *švejkovina*, which means behaving like Švejk. But that's completely different from *kafkárna*."

She notices that people in Czechoslovakia often compare something specific with something that they say doesn't exist at all, or that they don't know anything about it.

An office worker gives her an example: "Imagine you're

a man, you go into a store and ask if they've got any fleecy socks. The sales assistant replies: 'Ladies', yes—but we haven't got any for children.' That logic makes no sense, Miss, but it works."

"Where's the logic in that?"

"Because it assumes he knows, or ought to know, that men's socks haven't been on sale for the past six months, so there probably aren't any. So what socks can he be asking about? Obviously just ladies' or children's."

The student has over a hundred answers, but no proper definition.

The Charles University employees who come into contact with her are cagey. When, at a reception given in her honor, more and more people find out who she wants to write about, they all drop her like a hot potato.

However, the wives of her academic colleagues are braver than their husbands. The wife of the head of the institute for Czech literature admits to Buchanan that her husband is thinking of reading a little of that Kafka, but for the time being he can't. He started, but he can't get to the end. "Just imagine, he tried reading about the man who turned into an insect. But that's so unnatural, so dreadful. It's more like something from your American literature—you've got science fiction over there, haven't you?"

"Yes, we do."

"But in the Czech literary tradition, that sort of aberration is not at all usual."

The wife of another employee, the archivist at the institute, wants to set up the American student with her son, who hasn't a clue about Kafka. The mother decides to read *The*

Trial and summarize it for him, so he can impress his future
fiancée with it. She soon gives in to despair. She keeps going
back to the beginning of the book, because she thinks she's
missed the bit saying what Josef K. has been accused of. Then
she thinks she'll find out at the end, but still there's nothing.
Then she's convinced the writer must have coded the explanation into the subtext, but she still can't find it.

All this makes her erupt: "Son, it's a total fraud! There are
no clues! This book is supposed to be a horror story, but after
this many pages anyone reading a horror story should know
what they're supposed to be scared of!"

Two months later, two plainclothes police officers turn up
at the student's room. The Security Service wants to know if
the passers-by who replied to her survey hadn't by any chance
been deprived of their own will. And whether they had answered her questions in that state.

One of the professors advises the American that it would
be better not to use the name Kafka in her paper on Kafka.
He tries to convince her that in Czechoslovakia people are
extremely good at skirting boggy ground. "People have been
talking about the first Czechoslovak republic for years and
years, and sometimes they say the president of the time did
this or that. Everyone knows who they're talking about, but
no one ever says the name Masaryk, not for love or money.
And that's perfectly all right." So she'd better say "the writer."

It's 1992.

The story of Joy Buchanan wasn't written by me, but was
made up by an associate professor of American literature at

Charles University, Radoslav Nenadál. The son of an army officer, born in 1929, nowadays he is one of the leading translators from English. He wrote his novel *In the Footsteps of K.* in 1987, during the socialist era, and submitted it to a publisher. By some miracle, the employees at his institute knew what was in it before it was published. None of them spoke to him for over six months.

These experts on literature were all deeply offended by its content. They realized that the story was made up, and yet, as one of them commented, it was a truthful fabrication.

The publisher didn't dare publish it. It only came out in 1992, once socialism had collapsed, and the author had already retired. It was published by the Franz Kafka Publishing House, but they were unable to sell it. "Maybe people weren't ready for this sort of mockery?" the author wonders. So there are piles of his novel lying in the bargain bookstores. These days, the price per copy is the same as for a tram ticket.

"If you'd like to translate it into Polish," he says, "or at least summarize it in one of your journals, maybe it would leave more of a mark."

"By all means."

THE MOVIE HAS TO BE MADE

47

The SS *Marine Tiger* is sailing from Southampton to New York. Jarka (short for Jaroslava) Moserová from Prague is sitting beside Šárka Šrámková from Prachatice in a thirty-person cabin. She is describing how astonishing she finds her own family.

Jarka's grandmother addresses both her granddaughters in the informal second person, as "you," but addresses her own son and daughter in the third person, a form which is becoming old-fashioned. Jarka's grandfather calls his children "you," but his son calls him "sir." The son addresses his own sister in the third person, but talks to his mother informally as "you." "Would my daughter come here ..." "Has my son served himself some cake yet?" says Jarka, imitating her grandmother. "And no one knows where all this confusion comes from," she tells Šárka.

03

Zdeněk Adamec wakes up early and sees that there aren't any cheese sandwiches on his table yet. But Mom has already put out clean shorts for him (she ironed them last night), socks (ironed), and a thermos full of tea (sweetened). She has just run out to the store.

47

"And now I'll show you our pictures," says Jarka Moserová, fetching out the family photographs from her case to show Šárka.

In every single one, there is a middle-aged woman trying to escape. She is either turning her head away, or trying to shield it with a hand, or moving her entire buxom body out of the picture.

"That's Hilde, my favorite maid," says Jarka. "Whenever someone filmed her or took her picture, she ran off. We've got lots of movies with Hilde running away. She doesn't work for us anymore, because my sister and I grew up, and besides, she was a Sudeten German."

03

Zdeněk Adamec has P.E. today. Awkward.

Overweight. Sniggers. Sneering.

47

They sail into New York. Before the war, the Moser family subscribed to *National Geographic*, and Jarka sees that the American grass is exactly the same as in the pictures. So it wasn't lies—the grass really is darker than in Prague, it really does verge on blue.

From New York, they immediately take the train to Swannanoa in North Carolina. They are scholarship students sponsored by the American Field Service. The organization invites young people from countries which are under fascist occupation to visit schools. It is 1947, and the organization wants young Americans to hear from their contemporaries what it is like to live under threat.

The two girls enter the dining hall at the art school in gray woolen suits. The American girls are wearing long, loose shirts and denim dungarees. Jarka has never seen denim jeans before, or forks held unashamedly in the right hand.

03

The Adamec family's apartment is on the ground floor of a shabby block built in the 1970s. Last year, in June, Zdeněk planted five sunflowers under the window.

Once they had grown tall enough for him to see them from his room, two boys from the block came up one night and chopped them to pieces.

47

The head teacher at the American school suggests that Jarka enter her drawings and sculptures for an art competition in North Carolina.

In eight categories, Jarka wins seven first prizes and goes to Raleigh, the state capital, to collect seven Golden Keys. The eighth key is won by a black girl called Nora Williams. She is unsociable and hardly says a word. They are traveling home from Raleigh in the same direction. They board an empty bus, and Jarka wants her new friend to sit with her in the second row.

"I'm not allowed," says Nora. "Even if the bus is empty, we only have the right to sit in the back row. And only as many of us as can squeeze in at the back."

"Then I'm going to sit with you," says Jarka, and Nora gradually becomes more talkative.

During the journey, the whole bus turns to stare at the back. Finally, the situation is so tense that a passenger tells the driver to stop and sort it out.

"Are you black?" he asks Jarka.

Jarka thinks it's funny. "Of course I'm not," she replies.

She doesn't know she's not supposed to say that. Anyone who regards themselves as black is black. It's enough for them to have a single drop of black blood in their system. If she had said she was black, she would have been entitled to sit with Nora.

Two men get up from their seats, their faces are turning red, and they start breathing heavily. "I'm not black," says Jarka suddenly, "but I am from Czechoslovakia!"

And that remark saves her from a lynching.

03

Zdeněk Adamec switches on his cell phone. He knows all about phones. If a friend has an old, broken cell phone, even if it's in ten pieces, Zdeněk is the only person who can fix it for him. In a single afternoon, a cell phone can change people's minds about Zdeněk entirely. Tomorrow, they're all going to be reminded who Zdeněk really is anyway.

48

Out of the entire school, Jaroslava Moserová comes third in her final high-school exams. She should be on her way home to Czechoslovakia, but four months have gone by since February, when the communists took power there.

She reads that Czechoslovakia has refused American aid, in other words the Marshall Plan, and that the Soviet Union is its only friend. Even the symbol of democracy, government minister Jan Masaryk, has bitterly said of himself that he has become a Soviet lackey.

The head of the American school persuades Jarka that if she goes home, she will never leave the country again. He adds that as soon as she arrives in Prague, before being allowed to see her parents, she's sure to be sent to a re-education camp, because she is the granddaughter of the director general of a major investment bank.

At the camp, they will undoubtedly subject her to a change of consciousness.

03

Zdeněk's mom is sure he got up early to be at school an hour before classes.

49

The Americans have extended the Czechoslovak students' scholarships by a year, so Jaroslava Moserová is studying at the Art Students League. She earns a living at a lamp factory, where she paints roses in two colors onto the lamp stands.

In the spring, she finishes her studies and wants to earn the money for a trip. She is given a three-month post at the home of a manufacturer of dried-fruit vending machines. She will take care of his children. At their home on Long Island, there are already three black servants, including a cook. But no black hand is allowed to touch the children's beds, the children's bathroom or the children's clothes. "Of course, the children cannot enter the blacks' kitchen!" the machine manufacturer's wife explains to her. "You must make sure of that!"

03

At seven in the morning, they unlock the computer room at the industrial technical college in Humpolec, and every day before classes Zdeněk spends some time in there. He also spends time there after classes. Yesterday he was in a chat room until it was closed. He was chatting with Tomáš B., whose tag is *Cooldarebák*, meaning "Cool-rogue."

The topic was this: "I'm fat and I haven't got a girlfriend."

("So we were both fat guys," Cooldarebák will later say, "but he was the only one who didn't have a girlfriend.")

49

Jaroslava Moserová doesn't have complete faith in American civilization. In September, she wants to go home to her parents. She is nineteen now, and she decides that before being shut in a cage, she'll take a trip around the world. She sails on cargo ships from San Francisco to India, and then to Europe. She plays cards with the sailors, fails to make any real friends, and brings home parasols made of fish membrane which she bought in the Philippines.

On the train from Zurich to Prague, she is the only

passenger. Nobody is going into Czechoslovakia, and nobody is coming out of it.

She immediately wants to write to Nora Williams, but she realizes that in Czechoslovakia you don't write letters abroad. That is, you can write them, because there's freedom and the people's democracy, but nobody wants to do that.

Why not?

Because you don't know what sort of an answer you might get.

Someone once wrote back from Canada: "You've never liked red, and now what?" and this harmed not just the woman who got the letter, but her entire family. A journalist from Prague wrote a letter to the *Times* about how much the price of cigars had risen, and how the stores named *Lahůdky* ("Delicatessen") had been changed to *Pramen* ("Source"), and he was tried as a spy.

No, she won't be studying fine arts. Who knows whom they might order her to sculpt?

"But I'm going to be a plastic surgeon, Daddy. I'll make use of my talent, and surely they're not going to tell me to remodel my patients' faces to look like Marx and Engels?"

03

Zdeněk Adamec is getting dressed.

His father makes gravestones, and in Humpolec, a town of eleven thousand in the central Czech Republic, he is known for it. His mom is on a state allowance and devotes herself to her son. Right up to the sixth grade in elementary school, she used to walk him to school and come to fetch him. The head teacher noted at the time that it was the only case he knew of where a mother carried a schoolbag for a healthy thirteen-year-old boy. He shared his observation at a meeting of the school board.

"It looks to me as if the woman sticks to her son in an unhealthy way," he said.

51

By now, even students are obliged to address their teachers as "comrade."

As clerks at a state bank, Jaroslava's mom and uncle go to a community action event where everybody addresses each other as "comrade."

"And you know what, Jarka," her mom says afterwards, "in front of those people my brother didn't dare to ask, in the third person as usual: 'Would my sister like something to eat?' We stopped addressing each other normally! We started to feel embarrassed, so we spoke to each other impersonally, saying 'one could have something to eat,' or 'one will have a bite to eat later.' It's not as if we called each other 'comrade,' but we did come to a sort of compromise. Does making this sort of small compromise gradually lead to making big ones?"

03

Apparently, one of the teachers had said (though not in Zdeněk's presence) that his mother did things for him which every other boy does for himself.

Because his surname is Adamec, the boys call Zdeněk "Ada." "Ada!" they shouted recently. "We know your mom even spanks your monkey for you!"

Zdeněk went blue and stopped breathing.

51

Jarka's father, Jaroslav Moser, has four weaknesses: his wife, skiing, good cars and blondes. He is not in the Party. Nevertheless, as a lawyer and iron-working expert, he becomes a manager at a mining and steelworks syndicate in Ostrava. For unknown reasons, its Party-member boss commits suicide in his small garden, and Jaroslava's father is arrested. He gets out after a year. With no charges brought against him, no trial and no day in court.

Though haggard and deprived of a job, he is always happy about something. He says that in prison he sang arias from Wagner's operas. ("And if I hadn't ended up in there, it never would have occurred to me to sing.") He finds a job as a clerk at an incineration plant. He is proud that Jarka is studying surgery, and her older sister gynecology.

03

Zdeněk prefers leaving the block in the morning to coming back in the afternoon. In the morning, no one is playing soccer in the yard yet, and there's no fear of a ball accidentally flying towards him. Whenever he sees a ball coming his way, which he's supposed to kick back, he feels himself go weak.

(Later—once it's all over—one of the internet chat-room users will recall that Zdeněk confided in him that he was afraid of the ball because he couldn't kick it straight. "It's awful when a ball comes flying at me.")

55

Jarka Moserová is looking forward to receiving her diploma. She has no opportunity to read the thoughts of a writer from Poland on life under communism in a chapter entitled: "How do you go through university without losing faith in life?" (The Polish author's answer is that it can't be done.)

In the fifth year of her studies at Charles University, Jaroslava Moserová finds out that she won't get the title "doctor of medicine." The college authorities inform her: "The Party and the government have decided that graduates of the medical faculties throughout the country won't be called doctors of medicine, but 'graduate physicians.'"

A student delegation goes to see the president of the republic with a petition. They explain that patients will react badly to this, and it will reduce a doctor's authority.

The next day, all the students are summoned to the auditorium. The deputy minister of education and the head of the president's office make speeches. The chairman of the student delegation reports that the comrade president listened to their petition and said: "In principle I agree with you, but ..."

At this, the head of the president's office stands up and says that it isn't true: The comrade president said, "In principle I do not agree with you, but ..."

At that, the chairman of the delegation glances at his

fellow students, who handed in the petition with him, and says: "But I have witnesses!"

A couple of weeks before their graduation ceremony, the chairman shows his fellow students from the medical faculty a summons from the Security Service. On the sheet of paper, there is a charge: "Falsely misrepresenting the words of the Head of State."

He goes to the interrogation and disappears.

He is simply nowhere to be found, and nobody ever hears of him again.

The entire fifth year class in Medicine sits and waits for the graduation ceremony in silence.

Nobody is surprised by anything.

"Why are we keeping quiet?" wonders Jarka.

"Maybe because too many people keep disappearing," says a friend.

03

If Zdeněk goes anywhere after classes, it's with his mother, to polish the hood of the car.

Of course, his parents know the boy should have somewhere to go. They persuaded him to join a fishing club. Fishing and beer are two hobbies for real men in the Vysočina region. Zdeněk did go to the club for two years, and his father even joined it too.

And to improve things for Zdeněk, his father made an effort and became chairman of the club.

60

Now Jaroslava Moserová works in the burns unit at the Charles University hospital in Prague.

Her life includes an increasing number of the sort of incidents where all you can say is: "Oh ... my ... God!"

Mr. J. was a typographer, but he committed a mortal sin: he had his own printing press. In this situation, the Party decided that he would become an electrician.

They took away his printing works and told him to get used to his new profession. A month later, he was electrocuted so badly that he lost his brow, nose and cheekbones, and his eyeballs melted.

"Just imagine," Jaroslava tells her sister, "the current damaged his brain but in a merciful way."

"What do you mean, in a merciful way?" wonders her sister.

"Just slightly," explains Jarka, "so for a long time he remained in a state of—how can I put it?—misplaced optimism. He told me he'd go back to printing, so I started encouraging him to learn Braille. But he wouldn't hear of it! He said that these days, when man is getting ready to fly to the moon, doctors will soon know how to transplant eyes. And not only did the man saying this have no eyes, Boženka, he had no face either!

"Our professor made him an artificial face, modeled a nose, and was getting ready to give him eye sockets. So that glass eyes could be put in them. Then, if Mr. J. put on a pair of spectacles, nobody would realize ...

"And before doing the eye sockets, we let him go home. Because it was the summer vacation, and his daughter said he'd be able to rest in a fragrant garden. Just imagine, despite being completely blind, Mr. J. installed all the electricity in the house his daughter had just built! And to finish it off he put a TV aerial on the roof himself."

"That's wonderful!" says her delighted sister, who has no gynecological stories as spectacular as that one.

"But once the house was finished and the vacation ended, when the grandchildren had gone back to school and the daughter to work, Mr. J. was left on his own. And you know what? They came home one afternoon, and found him in the yard, dead. He hanged himself."

03

Zdeněk Adamec can't live without the Internet.

Yesterday, for instance, he looked at some websites about the mindless pollution of the global environment. He left a comment: "Mankind horrifies me."

He left traces on websites where there is proof that democracy is ineffective. ("Because it just means being ruled by civil servants and money," he added.)

He left traces on sites for supporters of the view that television is a tool of the devil.

He left them on sites for people who object to *Tom and Jerry* cartoons. ("These apparently innocent cartoons contain more violence than any others.")

On sites which predict a major energy crisis, to be followed by the outbreak of several wars over the remaining crude oil. ("That was the only reason for the attack on Iraq.")

On some chat sites and in some addresses, Zdeněk hides

behind the name "Satanic." (Afterwards, some people will claim that Adamec was also "Satanic666," whose comments were more aggressive.)

He agonizes over the imperfection of human nature. "What do we need the law for?" he asks. "Isn't each person capable of understanding what's allowed and what isn't? Evidently, we're not a mature civilization yet, and we have some learning to do."

60

For once in their lives, Jaroslava's parents are going abroad. At the invitation of their former maid, Hilde. She and her gynecologist husband live in West Germany. They greet each other. She with a sense of shame for the war, and they for the expulsion of the Sudeten Germans.

"It's like a scene from a movie, Boženka," Jaroslava tells her sister, "two impoverished old people going to see their maid, who receives them in a beautiful apartment. And all three are in tears."

Her sister shows her some photographs of her friends. In a group picture, Jaroslava sees a man and a boy, neither of whom she has ever met.

Her sister explains that the man is a lawyer called Milan David, and the boy is his son Tomáš. The man is divorced, and has custody of the twelve-year-old boy.

"I like that," she says, "a man with a ready-made child."

They go skiing with the people from the photo. Jaroslava takes cans of soup from Milan and sets them next to her own can on the electric cooker. After a week, they feel as if they belong to each other, and two years later they get married.

Milan and Tomáš live in a single room with Milan's father, also known as Grandpa Josef. The proposal goes like this: "Grandpa and Tomáš would love you to come and live in our room with us," says Milan.

Before the communists came to power, Grandpa—in other words, Milan's father—was the chairman of parliament. The day after the putsch he withdrew from politics, and for the past twelve years he has been solving crosswords. Now the chairman of parliament will sleep behind a curtain stretched on a string between the closet and the wall.

03

His mother notices that Zdeněk takes a backpack full of books.

So far, the head of the technical college has been very pleased with Zdeněk. In fact, he isn't doing well at Czech and P.E., but he's very good at physics and math. And he already knows all about computers. He was even going to offer him a paid job taking care of the Internet room, if not for that surprising incident with the police.

The police had discovered that Zdeněk Adamec was advising Internet users on how, for example, to make themselves a permanently charged payphone card.

There is also evidence indicating that Zdeněk Adamec lent access codes to his sites to alter-globalists. They used them to promote a method of interrupting the electricity supply. In order, obviously, to break the monopoly of the all-powerful capitalist state.

After his first police interview, Zdeněk immediately removed the websites.

63

One day, Jaroslava Moserová sees Czechoslovakia's most famous plastic surgeon, Professor František Burian, and cannot believe that he is smaller than she is. Standing on her right leg, she is only five foot six and a half inches tall, on her left five foot five and a half and on both five foot six.

"You've seen the smallest giant ever born," one of the associate professors explains to her.

Professor Burian is small, but he has a great big idea: the Atlas of Plastic Surgery. He wants it to have 850 illustrations, and in addition the drawings are to show real patients, which has apparently never happened before in the field of illustrated reference books. The professor will not allow any anonymous faces to be included. He provides old photographs and descriptions of operations, and Jaroslava Moserová, junior surgeon and member of the artists' union, spends four years illustrating the atlas.

The professor wears a hearing aid. Whenever he finds Jaroslava boring, he switches it off and starts to whistle. He is constantly dissatisfied. He makes her re-draw each illustration several times. After a while, before each meeting begins he asks her: "Are we going to have coffee first, or quarrel?"

She always prefers to quarrel first.

The housekeeper serves them the coffee. Professor Burian

lives with his daughter, his son-in-law and the home help. The housekeeper leaves when, for unknown reasons, the professor's son-in-law is arrested. The professor probably understands her; even in a dentist's waiting room, friends won't sit next to the family of someone who's been arrested. People are entitled to be afraid. Now the professor's daughter brings in the coffee.

Professor Burian won't live to see the atlas published; he'll die only two days after writing the introduction.

03

There are computer printouts lying on Zdeněk Adamec's desk. They are about Torch Number One.

Last year, Zdeněk started reading about an unusual student. He was known as Torch Number One. If, in August 1969, an exceptionally nasty era hadn't begun, if the Soviets and four other armies hadn't invaded the country, and if they hadn't become more and more tyrannical, Torch Number One wouldn't have had to resort to extreme measures.

Because, first of all, people gave in, and then they sold out. They were no longer allowed to say things that during the Spring were said freely. Torch Number One was a student in the philosophy faculty. He wanted to wake them up.

Zdeněk found the statement of a female student from Prague who later became a world-famous director, saying that the choice of those who were to be the top ten for self-immolation was made with great care. The point was for good students to set themselves on fire, young people who didn't have psychiatric problems, neuroses or broken hearts, so it wouldn't be possible for the propaganda to disavow the motives for their act. The best of the best were chosen. And then they drew lots.

Zdeněk read the letter written by Torch Number One before his death: "If our demands—including the lifting of censorship—are not met in the next five days, that is, by January 21, 1969, and if the nation does not additionally support them through a general strike, the next torches will burn."

Signed, "Torch Number One."

Zdeněk takes these printouts with him.

65

At the burns unit, mirrors are not allowed in the patients' rooms.

Not all the patients want their nearest and dearest to look at them. They would prefer to talk to them from behind screens.

Dr. Jaroslava Moserová collects material for her book *Skin Loss and Compensating for It*. She is interested in burned skin.

In places where skin has been charred, the patient's own skin is grafted, for the time being. It is cut out, stretched to a scale of one to three, and applied. Where there is a lack of the patient's own skin, for a couple of weeks skin from dead bodies is applied, like a natural dressing. But, in a few years' time, before Jaroslava Moserová finishes her book, a method of supplementing losses using skin from piglets will be developed. Pig skin is the most similar to human skin, closer than that of chimpanzees.

In the field of skin-loss compensation, Jaroslava Moserová

collaborates with some Polish scientists, who award her a gold medal.

She is also granted a scholarship to go to the University of Texas at Galveston.

She notices that she suffers from a strange affliction: she has no memory of the patients whom she has helped. She only remembers the ones in whose cases she failed.

Being ineffective is what she finds most horrifying about herself.

03

Mom asks if he took the sandwiches.

Zdeněk knows that Torch Number One bought a white plastic bucket somewhere in downtown Prague, and then filled it up at a gas station. He's not going to take a canister with him, because Mom will immediately ask what it's for. He too will buy himself a container in Prague.

He has already composed a letter, which begins with the words: "Dear Citizens of the World . . ." He posted it on a website called www.pochodnia2003.cz.*

69

A wave of burn victims injured during clashes with Soviet tanks has already passed through the unit.

On January 16, Jaroslava Moserová is on call when they

---

* The name of the site now is www.pochoden2003.nazory.cz. *Pochodnia* means "a torch."

bring in a young man. She hears the paramedics saying that this is Torch Number One. His name is Jan Palach. He set himself on fire outside the museum on Wenceslas Square. Almost the entire surface of his body is charred, as are his airways.

The orderlies, who always call young people by their first names, address him as "sir."

The nurses say he is Jan the Second, because he wanted to remind people of Jan Hus.

Jan Palach's death throes last for seventy-two hours.

People bring hundreds of flowers to the hospital for him, and hundreds of letters arrive. The nurses read the letters to him. Jaroslava Moserová reads them too. And in his fever, he opens his eyes and asks in a hoarse, suffering voice: "It wasn't in vain, was it?"

"No, it wasn't," they reply.

"That's good," says the patient.

The secret police are standing outside the hospital.

Despite the Soviet occupation, the coffin is set out in the hall of Charles University's Karolinum building, and there are candles in apartment windows. Crowds of people weep as they come to visit the deceased until midnight. All over the country, there are labor strikes, hunger strikes and rallies.

The funeral is a demonstration, and the grave in Prague's Olšany cemetery is a site of pilgrimage.

A few years later, the authorities force Palach's mother and brother to sign an exhumation agreement; then they remove the remains at night, cremate them, and give the urn to the family.

They will keep it at home, because the cemetery in Palach's native town of Všetaty refuses to accept it for a year.

In 1990, President Václav Havel will ceremonially return the urn from Všetaty to Olšany.

03

Zdeněk has a choice: he can travel from Humpolec to Prague by bus or by train. If he went by rail, he would have to change trains and would only get there in the afternoon. In Kolín, he would have to board the express train "Jan Palach." So he takes a direct bus, leaving at 6:30.

The road to Prague is a freeway—fifty-six miles down a narrow pass running between trees and meadows. What could have stopped him on this road? The only things visible, apart from the dark brown woods, still without leaves, are gigantic billboards saying: "Now's the time! Follow your heart. Get the benefit of a facelift."

"It's the right time to make a good investment. The New Phone Book..."

"Let me get my clothes off—0-800..."

Fifty minutes later, Zdeněk is in Prague.

76

After patients injured by the invasion, patients injured by the normalization start to appear—the first victims of the process of creating the new, obedient man. Mr. K., for example, one of 750,000 people who after 1970 are forced to change jobs.

Mr. K., who went to university and speaks three languages, was employed in foreign trade. The Party decided that he would lay asphalt on the streets. One day, a tank valve couldn't withstand the pressure and boiling tar came shooting out, straight at Mr. K.

It melted his entire body apart from his face.

People who deal with monstrosities have to find ways to prevent themselves from going mad.

For example, at first Jaroslava Moserová used to draw different versions of a little girl walking along with a sunflower held high.

Now she is protected from madness by Dick Francis—the Queen Mother's top jockey.

He competed in the Grand National, riding the Queen Mother's favorite, a horse called Devon Loch. The entire royal family was sure he would win. Suddenly, on the final straight the horse fell. Then it seemed to come to its senses, got up and ran on, but it could no longer win. Afterwards, it was examined—it wasn't injured or sick. For years, people debated this astonishing incident, although the Queen Mother was typically stoical about it, commenting: "Oh, that's racing!"

And the demoted Dick Francis wrote a novel in which it featured.

Then he started thinking up detective stories. Most of his novels are set at the horse races, and Jaroslava Moserová translates them all into Czech.

By 2003, she had translated forty-four of his novels, and won a prize for the art of translation, while in the Czech Republic Dick Francis has outsold Agatha Christie herself.

"What helps you to unwind?" ask the journalists. "Why

do you translate these particular books? And why only this author?"

"Because good always triumphs in them, and evil is punished. Apart from that, he's reluctant to send anyone to jail," replies Jaroslava Moserová.

"If a bad guy does have to be punished, he's more likely to fall off a cliff or get killed in a crash," she adds.

It's the 1970s, and the word "jail" puts the Czechoslovak journalists on their guard; maybe they'd rather not see it in print, so they'd like her to give them a different reason.

"Well, all right," the translator does her best to satisfy them, "I also like the fact that in his books the only person who has to try and think up an alibi is the murderer."

03

Mrs. Adamcová calls Zdeněk on his cell phone. She called earlier, but he didn't pick up. "Where are you, son?" she asks.

"Where do you think?" replies Zdeněk, and hangs up.

77

To Jaroslava Moserová, Václav Havel is the small boy in short pants, standing next to her and her sister Božena in a photograph. Their families were friends. The girls are about seven and nine years old, and Havel is three.

Her stepson looks at the photo and asks: "What did you and your sister talk to Mr. Havel about, Mom?"

"Nothing, Tomáš!" says his stepmother indignantly. "We took no notice of him at all. He was too young for us."

03

Zdeněk Adamec has a full canister now.

87

Apparently, Jaroslava Moserová has treated a patient who suffered burns in a gas explosion, affecting not just the flesh under his thick shorts, but his hands too, because he had them in his pockets. He is a young violinist, and before the explosion he studied at the conservatory. A year after the skin graft he has started to practice again, but he can't stand and hold the bow in his hand for long. After only ten minutes, he loses heart. As his doctor comes from a home where the children had to know the difference between Monet and Manet, and play the piano, she starts practicing with him, playing duets by Corelli.

To catch up with the qualified violinist, the surgeon in her fifties signs up for piano lessons. When they practice together, the boy can keep going for a whole hour.

They play like that for three years.

Then they appear at the Congress of the European Society of Plastic Surgeons, where they perform Janáček.

Now Jaroslava Moserová has an idea for a screenplay.

A mother has unintentionally injured her daughter's cheek. The story begins when the girl is already grown up; she has a scar on her beautiful face, a good job and lots of friends. Everything is fine, except for the mother's sense of guilt. She plagues her daughter by being morbidly overprotective. Guilt is her life.

The screenplay idea appeals to Evald Schorm, an icon of the Czechoslovak New Wave in cinema who has been silent for almost twenty years, roughly since the death of Palach. He wants to direct it, but he has no desire to write the script. He says she should write it. When Jaroslava tries to make excuses, Schorm explains how to write it: everything that's heard, such as a car hooting, goes on the left-hand side of the script, and everything that's seen, such as a curtain moving, goes on the right.

The role of the mother will be played by a friend of Jaroslava's. She is the ex-wife of the nice orphan boy who used to visit the Mosers after the war. He had nobody, and he wanted someone to spread butter on his bread, and even to shout at him now and then, which is understandable—what he needed was a substitute family. The actress friend is called Jana Brejchová, and the name of her former husband with the bread and butter is Miloš Forman.

The movie is going to happen, but it can't have the title the screenwriter wants. She'd like it to be called *White Lie*.

The word "lie," like the word "truth," is banned in art, and during the normalization neither of them can be used. Another iconic director of the Czechoslovak New Wave, Věra Chytilová, has been unable to use the words "I think" in a movie. "I think that . . ." the actor said quite slowly, but the pre-screening inspection committee ruled that he shouldn't think so meaningfully, because that could be interpreted in various ways. And at another point, when a man locked himself in the bathroom and shouted, "I'm trapped," Věra Chytilová had to cut the entire scene out of the movie.

So Evald Schorm's latest picture is called *Nothing Really Happened.*

03
Zdeněk Adamec goes up the wide museum steps.

It's eight in the morning and it's cold, at the beginning of March.

89
Seriously ill, Evald Schorm dies a month before the premiere of the movie.

Coincidentally, it is scheduled for January 19, at the movie theater in the Lucerna Palace on Wenceslas Square.

But that day, no trams or subway trains are running there. It was on January 19 twenty years ago that Jan Palach died, and in the square several thousand demonstrators have just been surrounded by militiamen.

There is no audience at all for the premiere of *Nothing Really Happened.*

In May, *Gazeta Wyborcza* comes out for the first time in Poland—the country's first independent newspaper—but in Czechoslovakia, Václav Havel is still in jail. But by November, when the Civic Forum is formed, he is at the head of it. Actors, philosophers, journalists and doctors join ... She joins too. "But I have lots of fears—after all, I'm not a politician," she says.

"Thank God, Mrs. Moserová, none of us are politicians," her colleagues reassure her.

03

Just like Torch Number One, Zdeněk Adamec soaks himself, from the head down.

He jumps onto the stone balustrade and fires up a cigarette lighter.

He leaps.

Contact with the air in motion causes the fire to engulf his entire body evenly.

01

Seventy-one-year-old Jaroslava Moserová writes her memoirs, *Stories: People You Never Forget*. She sets up www. moserova.cz, as she needs to account for the past twelve years.

She has been vice president of the Civic Forum, Czechoslovakia's and then the Czech Republic's ambassador to Australia and New Zealand, and vice president of the Senate of the Czech Republic.

She has also been president of the General Conference of UNESCO, which supports education. Jaroslava Moserová believes there are simple ways to help even the poorest parts of the world. If there aren't enough resources for education, the first thing you need to do is set up a radio station. The radio will be an attraction, and at the same time it can teach people about hygiene and birth control.

Now Moserová is a senator for the ODA, or Civic Democratic Alliance, representing the Pardubice constituency. The ODA competes with Václav Klaus's Civic Democratic Party.

Her party doesn't have huge support. So what if they wanted to reduce annual tax returns to a single sheet of A4?

(People liked that.) So what if they wanted to register same-sex partnerships? (Not everybody liked that.) When at the same time they wanted complete exemption from paying rent. (Hardly anybody liked that!)

Jaroslava Moserová only won because people in Pardubice reckoned she was a decent woman.

03

Zdeněk Adamec falls four yards away from the spot where Palach set himself on fire.

His lips are burned, but he is still trying to say something.

Later it will be reported that, like Torch Number Two—Jan Zajíc—Zdeněk Adamec drank corrosive acid to stop himself from screaming.

02

Now and then, Jaroslava Moserová comes up against a certain issue.

It concerns the fact that in 1977 she did not sign a document which was very important for any decent person to sign. Especially as the campaign and the document were initiated by the boy in the photograph, the one in short pants, who thirty-six years earlier had been too young for a serious conversation with the Moserová sisters.

Why didn't she sign Charter '77?

Jaroslava Moserová could give an answer in the style of Bohumil Hrabal: "I have so much trouble dealing with myself, and so much trouble with my own friends and relatives that I haven't enough time to follow changing political events in any way. I don't even know what the people who want those changes are talking about, because the only thing I would want to change is myself."

She could say something of the kind, as Hrabal did, and she would probably be understood.

But Jaroslava Moserová says: "If the Charter had come to me, I certainly would have signed it, but as it didn't come, I didn't go looking for it.

"So I admit: I was being cautious."

At the suggestion of a rather overly self-confident journalist from Poland that a person is only what he pretends to be, and it's impossible for her nowadays as a politician and diplomat never to have told a lie, Jaroslava Moserová replies that there are situations in which a politician cannot always tell the entire truth, but he should never tell a lie.

At least in her opinion.

As she's always done—for decades—she goes to church.

In the Senate, they say she is quite appalled by Klaus, who said a while back that for him the Church is the same sort of organization as a walking club.

03

Zdeněk Adamec is lying in a pool of water, doused by the firefighters, and the temperature is below freezing.

People stand there helplessly. None of the curious onlookers calls an ambulance.

Three doctors only come after a call from the firefighters. They carry him to an ambulance.

He lives for another thirty minutes.

03

Jaroslava Moserová tells a friend that Milan, Tomáš and the grandchildren are the best things that have ever happened to her. She tells her family she has decided to stand as president of the country.

She prepares a speech to give to parliament: "I know that dishonesty is what offends young people the most. And they blame us, the politicians, for the rise of immorality. In a way, they are right ..."

And she ends it like this: "In our country, politicians aren't trusted. I hope this will change. Please have trust in me."

The serious press isn't interested in her. Not a single analysis of her electoral chances or her views is published, and nobody does a major interview with her.

But a journalist from a women's glossy magazine tells a reporter from Poland that the candidate, as a plastic surgeon, could have far fewer wrinkles than she does.

After all, an interview in her magazine has to have a really stunning picture to go with it!

03

Senator Jaroslava Moserová hears about the death of Zdeněk Adamec a month after losing the election.

She is sitting in the conference room at Wiston House in Wilton Park, Great Britain. She's taking part in a world anti-corruption conference.

She opens her laptop, logs on to www.pochodnia2003.cz, and reads:

My whole life has been a complete failure. I feel as if I don't fit in with the times. As I am just another victim of the System, I have decided my suffering is going to end for good. I can't go on anymore. Other people aren't interested. They're indifferent. And the politicians are like little lords who trample on ordinary people. I want everyone to stop and think about themselves and limit the evil they commit each day. You'll find out the rest about me from the press afterwards.

And the final sentence of the letter: "Don't portray me as a madman." Jaroslava Moserová closes her computer. The thought that occurs to her is that none of the countries here at the world anti-corruption conference has presented a sensible remedy for it.

03

The press notes that in his farewell letter the boy did not make a single mention of his parents.

A famous writer points out that Zdeněk Adamec's sacrifice is like a repetition of Jesus' sacrifice.

A famous bishop writes that, on reading Zdeněk's

statement, we would instantly like to label his story as "pathology." Unfortunately, this is just the tip of the iceberg. The iceberg is a sense of pointlessness among the younger generation.

Next day, people lay flowers and messages at the site of the suicide. They burn votive candles.

They also lay flowers and light candles for Palach.

Foreign tour groups line up to have both islands of flowers visible in their photographs.

Unfortunately, there is some resulting confusion. At the site of Palach's death, messages appear saying: "Zdeněk, you're right!"

03

On the evening of the third day, there's a gantry standing by the museum steps. A crew is fitting it with television spotlights.

It's as bright as day.

The cameras are on standby.

There's a crowd of people. Right in the middle stand three men in smart black overcoats, who have just got out of a car. One of them is holding flowers.

Everything is ringed with red-and-white tape. A policeman is keeping watch to make sure nobody crosses it.

There's an atmosphere of anticipation. "There's going to be a broadcast about that boy," the passers-by explain to each other, and each of them cranes his neck as high as possible.

They ask the policeman for details. "Is it a ceremony? In honor of that Zdeněk guy from Humpolec?"

"Zdeněk who, sir?" says the policeman. "They're making a biopic about Hitler here. The Canadians are filming it."

"But this spot was covered in flowers and candles. What happened? Have they put out the vigil lights? Removed them? Three days after his death, that's awful!"

"Nobody put them out," the policeman explains patiently. "Take a look over here, please—they've shielded the candles behind a car, so they won't appear in the film. As you know, a contract's a contract, this sort of movie can't be called off. A movie's a movie, sir. The movie has to be made."

METAMORPHOSIS

It is March 27, 2003.

The Komedia Theater in Prague (with the Tragedia Café inside it) presents Franz Kafka's *Metamorphosis*, directed by Arnošt Goldflam.

In this staging, the main character's problem is not that he has changed into an insect, but how he's going to go to work in this state.

GOTTLAND'S LIFE AFTER LIFE

In 2007, when *Gottland* was published in the Czech Republic, someone demanded that it be pulped.

It wasn't the general public, or the authorities of course, but a representative of the Gottland museum.

The Czech publisher received a summons to stop selling the book immediately and to withdraw it from bookstores. The Gottland museum sent letters to all the wholesalers in the Czech Republic, warning them that it was illegal to sell this book "because it's against the principle of competition—the word *Gottland* is exclusively reserved for Karel Gott's museum."

In the entire Czech Republic, this appeal only upset one bookseller in Ostrava, who hid the book in his storeroom, and on his website replaced the title *Gottland* with *Gxxxxxxd*.

The Czech and Polish publishers declared that they weren't going to change the title, and decided to continue selling the book. For although you can patent a trademark, nobody can impose a ban on words used in literature. The book's title is a part of literature, which has to be free.

Faced with the publishers' uncompromising attitude, the museum withdrew its claims.

The bookseller in Ostrava put the book back on his shelves.

In August 2008, the owner of the Gottland museum, a

businessman called Jan Moťovský, who also owned the Gott restaurant, went missing while on a business trip to France.

In November 2009, after less than three years in operation, following a decision by the wife of the owner, who still hadn't been found, the Gottland museum was closed.

Souvenirs from the former museum can be bought on the website www.gottland.cz.

In 2006, the Czech president, Václav Klaus, did something for Karel Gott that perhaps no Polish president would ever agree to do for any artist. Out of admiration, he wrote the foreword for Gott's autobiography.

But that's nothing.

In his foreword, the president commented on Gott's sexuality. "I'm not disappointed as far as Karel Gott's potency is concerned," wrote Václav Klaus.

On an Internet chat site, the star once confessed to having had sex with 462 women (as of February 24, 2002). "And I had no desire to get married to all of them," he added.

When the president was due to award state decorations "For Merit," a group of parliamentary deputies across the political spectrum signed a petition calling on him to decorate Gott too, for "excellent representation of the Czech Republic worldwide."

The right-wing vice-chairman of parliament said that he didn't listen to Gott's music, but whenever he saw him, he simply had to take his hat off to him.

The left-wing minister of finance explained his signature on the petition in a single sentence: "He's my mom's favorite singer."

(However, I have a different explanation for the petition

signed by deputies of all parties: I think that, subconsciously, each of them respects Gott for his model sex life. Gott is a god to women, and in the Czech Republic even the men who don't like him respect him for this.)

In fall 2009, Karel Gott was awarded the "For Merit" medal.

Some Czech reviewers and readers have written to me or told me in person that the title *Gottland* is unfair to their country. They don't think of it as the land of Gott, and it's hard for them to swallow this piece of provocation.

So I started explaining at public events that Gottland can also be understood as God's land, which is best typified by a quotation from a poem by the Czech poet Vladimír Holan:

I don't know who does the Gods' laundry
I do know it's we who drink the dirty water

And that this should have been the book's motto, but I forgot to add it.

Strangely, I've noticed that this explanation reassures people who object to the title.

In 2002, Václav Neckář suffered a stroke. After several years of rehab, he managed to learn the words to some of his songs again.

In view of this, a decision was made to reunite the Golden Kids pop group.

Marta Kubišová, Helena Vondráčková and Václav Neckář got ready for a concert tour to mark the fortieth anniversary of the group's formation. The concerts were brought to a halt by a legal dispute between Vondráčková and Kubišová.

According to the press, Kubišová wasn't able to accept all the ideas proposed by Vondráčková's management, and as there was no written contract between them, she withdrew from preparations for the tour.

Helena Vondráčková's husband, who is her manager, demanded 1.3 million crowns (about U.S. $70,000) from Kubišová in compensation for the resulting losses, but after a court case, which went on for several years, the plaintiffs lost.

As somebody said, what matters is that communism failed to drive a wedge between the first lady of song and the national icon.

A reader from the Czech Republic wrote to tell me that the Czechs have been making beer for several hundred years, but they've forgotten that it's meant to have a bitter taste, and thanks me for reminding them about it with this book.

Patrik Ohera, a reader from Slovakia, informed me that there's a mistake in the book. The assassination of Reinhard Heydrich, Protector of Bohemia and Moravia, was not carried out by two Czechs, but by Jan Kubiš—a Czech from Dolní Vilémovice, and Jozef Gabčík—a Slovak from Poluvsie.

I replied that I had received several hundred emails from Czech readers, but not one of them had pointed this out to me.

"I don't want to look like a Slovak nationalist, but the fact that nobody has drawn your attention to this illustrates the relationship between Czechs and Slovaks. I have noticed that all sorts of things from the days of Czechoslovakia are described as Czech, though they were not," he wrote back.

Some readers from Chełmek, in southern Poland, who belong to a Bata fan club protested that I had only described the company on Czech terrain. Bata was active in Chełmek, where it built its own factories and housing, so they ask me to write my next book about Chełmek.

Despite this oversight, this book has its own monument in Chełmek. Or rather mini-monument, in the form of some concrete paving stones, which an artist called Magdalena Magdziarz has imprinted with text from the first chapter.

When efforts were being made for *Gottland* to appear on the French market, I heard that there were fears that it might not attract any readers. It wasn't certain if anyone in the West would be interested in what a Pole has to say about the Czechs. I could understand that—a representative of one marginal nation writing about another marginal nation is unlikely to be a success.

Yet Margot Carlier, the French translator, had faith in this book and was tenacious, for which I am extremely grateful to her.

So when *Gottland* won the 2009 Europe Book Prize, I said in my speech: "I'm pleased that a book by a Pole about the Czechs has been recognized as a European's book about Europe."

And that in the "prose" category (including fiction and nonfiction), fact had won over fabrication.

Besides, I get the impression that in today's world there's so much happening that there's no need to fabricate anything anymore.

ACKNOWLEDGMENTS

My thanks are due to my Czech friends and colleagues for their support, namely Tomáš Blahut, Václav Burian, Roman Chměl, Viola Fischerová, Adam Georgijev, Michal Ginter, Joanna Hornik, Pavel Janáček, Mirra Korytová, Alexej Kusák, Michal Nikodem, Štěpánka Radostná, Martin Skyba, Helena Stachová, Dalibor Statník and Pavel Trojan.

SOURCES

IV. sjezd Svazu československých spisovatelů. Praha 27.–29. června 1967. Protokol. Prague, 1968.

Alan, Josef, ed. *Alternativní kultura. Příběh české společnosti 1945–1989.* Prague, 2001.

Arcanjo, Francisco Moacir. *Svět porozumí. Příběh krále bot Jana Antonína Bati,* trans. Marek Belza. Krásna Lípa, 2004.

Ash, Timothy Garton. *History of the Present: Essays, Sketches and Despatches from Europe in the 1990s.* London, 1999.

Baarová, Lída. *Života sladké hořkosti.* Ostrava, 1998.

Bartošek, Karel. *Češi nemocní dějinami. Eseje, studie, záznamy z let 1968–1993.* Prague—Litomyšl, 2003.

Baťa, Jan A. *Spolupráce. Výbor z článků a projevů v letech 1920–1936.* Zlín, 1936.

Baťa, Tomáš J., and Soňa Sinclairová. *Švec pro celý svět.* Prague, 1991.

Benčík, Antonín, and Josef Domaňský. *21. srpen 1968.* Prague, 1990.

Brandes, Detlef. *Die Tschechen unter deutschem Protektorat. Teil II. Besatzungspolitik, Kollaboration und Widerstand im Protektorat Böhmen und Mähren von Heydrichs Tod bis zum Prager Aufstand (1942–1945).* Munich/Vienna, 1975.

Brož, Ivan. *Chlapi od Baťů. Osudy baťovců v době, kdy šéfoval Jan Baťa.* Prague 2002.

Cekota, Antonín. *Jak rostl Zlín: Naše volby 1923–1927.* Zlín, [date of publication unknown].

Černý, Václav. *Paměti 1945–1972.* Brno, 1992.

Dubček, Alexander. *Hope Dies Last: The Autobiography of Alexander Dubcek,* trans. Jiri Hochman. New York, 1993.

Dvořáková, Jiřina. *Bedřich Pokorný—vzestup a pád,* in "Sborník archivu Ministerstva vnitra," 2/2004. Prague, 2004.

Evžen, Erdély. *Baťa—švec, který dobyl světa.* Prague [1932], II ed. Bratislava, 1990.

Fabián, Karel. *Letící kůň.* Prague, 1961.

Georgiev, Adam. *Chytat slunce. Kniha o Martě Kubišové.* Prague, 1997.

Górny, Maciej. *Między Marksem a Palackým. Historiografia w komunistycznej Czechosłowacji.* Warsaw, 2001.

Grunberger, Richard. *A Social History of the Third Reich.* London, 1971.

Havel, Václav. *Living in Truth,* ed. Jan Vladislav. London, 1990.

———. *The Memorandum,* trans. Vera Blackwell, in: *Three East European Plays.* London, 1970.

Holan, Vladimír. *Terezka Planetová.* Prague, 1944.

Hrabal, Bohumil. *Zrada zrcadel,* in *Inzerát na dům, ve kterém už nechci bydlet.* Prague, 1965.

Ivanov, Miroslav. *Sága o životě a smrti Jana Bati a jeho bratra Tomáše.* Vizovice, 2000.

Janáček, Pavel. *Literární brak. Operace vyloučení, operace nahrazení 1938–1951.* Brno, 2004.

Janáček, Pavel, and Michal Jareš, *Svět rodokapsu. Komentovaný soupis sešitových románových edic 30. a 40. let 20. století.* Prague, 2003.

Jedlička, Josef. *České typy aneb Poptávka po našem hrdinovi.* Prague, 1992.

Jesenská, Milena. *Nad naše síly: Češi, židé a Němci 1937–1939,* ed. Václav Burian. Olomouc, 1997.

Jirous, Ivan M. *Magorův zápisník.* Prague, 1997.

Kaczorowski, Aleksander. *Praski elementarz.* Warsaw, 2001.

Kalenská, Renáta. *Rozhovory na konci milénia.* Prague, 2001.

Karlík, Viktor, and Terezie Pokorná. *Anticharta.* Prague, 2002.

Kocian, Jiří, and Jiří Pernes, Oldřich Tůma, a kol. *České průšvihy aneb Prohry, krize, skandály a aféry českých dějin let 1848–1989.* Brno, 2004.

Kohout, Pavel. *The Hangwoman,* trans. Káča Poláčková-Henley. New York, 1981.

———. *Z deníku kontrarevolucionáře aneb Životy od tanku k tanku.* Prague, 1997.

Kosatík, Pavel. *Fenomén Kohout*. Prague—Litomyšl, 2001.

Koschmal, Walter, and Marek Nekula, Joachim Rogall, ed. *Češi a Němci. Dějiny—kultura—politika*. Prague—Litomyšl, 2001.

Kroutvor, Josef. "Potíže střední Evropy: anekdota a dějiny," in *Potíže s dějinami*. Prague, 1990.

Kučera, Bohumil. *Batismus—ideologie sociálfašismu*. Gottwaldov, 1959.

Kunze, Reiner. *The Wonderful Years*, trans. Joachim Neugroschel. New York, 1977.

Lehár, Bohumil. *Přehledné dějiny n.p. Svít před znárodněním (1894–1945)*. Gottwaldov, 1959.

Miklaszewska, Maryna. *Drugie odejście barda*. "Karta" nr 20/1996.

Motl, Stanislav. *Prokletí Lídy Baarové*. Prague, 2002.

Nenadál, Radoslav. *Tudy chodil K.* Prague, 1992.

Pagáč, Jaroslav, ed. *Tomáš Baťa a 30 let jeho podnikatelské práce*. Prague, 1926.

Pokluda, Zdeněk. *Ze Zlína do světa—příběh Tomáše Bati*. Zlín, 2004.

Prečan, Vilém, ed. *Charta 77 (1977–1989). Od morální k demokratické revoluce. Dokumentace*. Bratislava, 1990.

Procházka, Jan. *Politika pro každého*. Prague, 1968.

Procházková, Lenka. *Děkovačka pro hrobníka*, in: *Evropský fejeton*. Brno, 1992.

"Ročenka Baťa 1940." Zlín, 1940.

Rybka, Zdeněk. *Základní zásady Baťova systému pro podnikatele a vedoucí pracovníky. Studie*. Prague, 1999.

Tigrid, Pavel. *Kapesní průvodce inteligentní ženy po vlastním osudu*. Prague, 2002.

Tomaszewski, Jerzy. *Czechosłowacja*. Warsaw, 1997.

Tomeš, Josef, a kol. *Český biografický slovník XX. století*. Prague, 1999.

Turek, Svatopluk. *Batismus v kostce*. Gottwaldov, 1950.

———. *Botostroj*. Prague 1946.

———. *Bude odsouzen zrádce J.A. Baťa?* Zlín, 1947.

———. *Pravá tvář batismu*. Prague, 1959.

———. *Zrada rodiny Baťovy*. Gottwaldov, 1949.

Vaculík, Ludvík. *Nepaměti (1969–1972)*. Prague, 1998.

Vaculíková, Madla. *Já jsem oves. Rozhovor s Pavlem Kosatíkem*. Prague, 2002.

Valach, František. *Fenomén Baťa*. Prague, 1990.

Vančura, Jiří. *Naděje a zklamání. Pražské jaro 1968*. Prague, 1990.

Vávra, Otakar. *Podivný život režiséra. Obrazy vzpomínek*. Prague, 1996.

Zelený, Milan. *Cesty k úspěchu. Trvalé hodnoty soustavy Baťa*. [Place of publication unknown], 2005.

ALSO

Material from Marta Kubišová's Prague fan club.

Annual editions of the periodicals: *Dikobraz, Rudé právo, Záběr, Reflex*, and *Respekt*.

Television documentary *Předčasná úmrtí*, dir. Jordi Niubó, Česká televize 2001.

INDEX OF NAMES

Note: Czech women's surnames have historically been formed from their father's or husband's surname with a suffix indicating a feminine gender. Thus: Lenka Procházková, the daughter of Jan Procházka; and Milena Jesenská, the daughter of Jan Jesenský.